16

The Evolution of Pension Systems in Eastern Europe and Central Asia: Opportunities, Constraints, Dilemmas and Emerging Practices

David Lindeman
Michal Rutkowski
Oleksiy Sluchynskyy

The World Bank
Washington, D.C.

The Evolution of Pension Systems in Eastern Europe and Central Asia: Opportunities, Constraints, Dilemmas and Emerging Practices

David Lindeman[*], Michal Rutkowski[**], and Oleksiy Sluchynskyy[***]

August 14, 2000[****]

Do not quote without permission

Abstract

Since the early 1990s the transition economy countries of Eastern Europe and Central Asia have had to adapt their pension systems in both minor and often very major ways. Some of the changes related to shrinking contribution bases and the inability to finance prior commitments, while still having to protect the pensioned populations from poverty. Other changes, however, reflected the need to make pension systems more sustainable in light of forthcoming demographic changes. The reforms entail a move away from a single pillar pay-as-you-go defined benefit systems toward multi-pillar systems that include a funded defined contribution component, and changes that convert remaining pay-as-you-go components into ones that are more self sustaining and transparent. The paper describes ongoing developments, assesses the effects of current and forthcoming challenges in light of potential labor market changes and examines choices for a new pensions system with respect to the organization, administration, guarantees, transition arrangements, participation requirements, role of the Government, annuitization etc. The paper concludes that though a "one size fits all" approach is clearly not appropriate, some practices emerging from the experiences in this region and elsewhere may offer useful guidance to others as they undertake deeper pension reforms.

---

[*] Adviser, Pensions, Social Protection Anchor Unit, The World Bank.

[**] Sector Manager, Social Protection, Europe and Central Asia Region, The World Bank; staff director of Polish Government office for pension reform, 1996-97.

[***] Japan/World Bank/KSG Fellow, Kennedy School of Government, Harvard University.

[****] The authors wish to acknowledge their colleagues whose analyses and writings contributed to the paper. Section one draws in part on Robert Palacios and Xiaoqing Yu's contributions to the pension reform strategy paper for Europe and Central Asia. Section three draws on advisory memoranda prepared for Estonia and Lithuania pension reform workshops, which included the experienced and insightful contributions of Agnieszka Chlon, Csaba Feher, Ardo Hansson, Zygmunt Kostkiewicz, Donald McIsaac, Kadi Oorn, Lawrence H. Thompson, Rafael Rofman and Xiaoqing Yu. The authors also wish to thank those who commented on earlier drafts, in particular Rhoda Davis, Estelle James, Louise Fox, Robert Holzmann, Robert Palacios, Aleksandra Posarac, Roberto Rocha, Anita Schwarz, Marcelo Selowsky and Asta Zviniene. The views and conclusions presented here are, however, the sole responsibility of the paper's authors and do not necessarily reflect official views of the World Bank and the Kennedy School of Government.

Please address e-mails and letters to Michal Rutkowski (MRUTKOWSKI@WORLDBANK.ORG).

Contents

Tables

Figures

The Evolution of Pension Systems in Eastern Europe and Central Asia:
Opportunities, Constraints, Dilemmas and Emerging Practices

This paper reviews how the pension systems of Eastern Europe and Central Asia (ECA) [1] responded to the new political and economic realities of the 1990s. All the countries in the region inherited state monopoly pay-as-you-go (PAYG) schemes that used conventional defined benefit (DB) formulas. The economic shocks of transition severely wrenched these systems, necessitating short-term adaptations of different degrees of severity. Equally important, the shocks heightened awareness that more profound restructuring will be needed to accommodate pending population bulges and likely demographic changes. Some countries have had to reconfigure their state systems to be basic safety nets for the aged and disabled populations. Other countries, better positioned at the outset of transition, have been able to reengineer their PAYG schemes in accord with prevailing views of equity and to improve labor and compliance incentives. In some instances, reforms have also included the introduction of "second pillars" based on funded defined contribution (DC) accounts.

In this paper, we (i) review how countries in the region have dealt and are dealing with the challenges of the 1990s; (ii) examine the deeper challenges in the future posed by demographics; and (iii) summarize some emerging practices with respect to the architecture of reformed systems, with particular emphasis on the design elements attendant on the introduction of a funded second pillars (relative sizes of the PAYG and funded pillars, financing the transition, participation requirements, guarantees, contribution collection and record-keeping, supervision, and such).

1. The ongoing changes

During the early transition period (1990-94), all the ECA countries had to react to pressures arising from shrinking contribution bases and growing beneficiary populations, both of which were caused by contractions in economic activity. In many countries, growing noncompliance has exacerbated the fiscal and policy challenges. Such was the depth of the economic shocks that in all countries the ongoing PAYG compacts had to be rewritten to some degree with some of the adjustment burden borne by retirees and older workers. In general, the better economically positioned the country was at the beginning of the transition, the more the beneficiary population was insulated from changes. All countries, however, had to modify indexing rules [2] for some period to control costs, usually away from a pre-existing norm of adjusting benefits in pay status according to nominal wage growth toward price indexing (or, more radically, in terms of what available resources would allow, even if less than price growth). The other key variable

---

[1] In this paper, when the phrase ECA is used, it excludes Turkey. In the World Bank the ECA region comprises economies with centrally planned economy heritage. Turkey, as the only exception, is not explicitly covered by this paper, although several findings, especially in section 3, will equally apply to Turkey.

[2] In this paper we use the word 'indexing' to mean adjustments to benefits in pay status. The word 'valorization' is used to cover adjustments to workers' wage histories that adjust for price and wage changes from a year in which a wage was earned to a period at or just before retirement.

3

nominal wage growth toward price indexing (or, more radically, in terms of what available resources would allow, even if less than price growth). The other key variable has been the retirement age. A few countries, such as Lithuania, were able during this period to begin raising effective retirement ages gradually. In one instance, Georgia, circumstances demanded that the retirement age had to be raised very precipitously.[3]

Some countries were able to use this initial period also to change benefit formulas, including increasing the reference period on which benefits are based, in order both to lower future promises and improve horizontal equity. To begin breaking the state PAYG monopoly some countries embarked on an expansion of voluntary private pension alternatives (typically with favorable tax treatment, or in the case of the Czech Republic, through matching payments from the national Budget), designed to allow and encourage households to do more consumption smoothing than can now be provided in the public pension schemes, and to diversify their retirement portfolio risks.

Despite a common heritage, by the middle of the 1990s, it was clear that two different groups had emerged within the ECA region. State pensions typically have the dual objectives of minimizing poverty among the aged and disabled and smoothing consumption among middle income households. Some countries in the region, especially those in Central Asia and the Caucasus, had to seriously compromise the consumption-smoothing objective in light of insufficient resources; maintaining a minimally adequate income floor became the overriding objective. Therefore, in early 2000, Georgia, Azerbaijan, Armenia, Tajikistan, Albania, Ukraine, among others, effectively have systems in which there is little or small differentiation among recipients according to earnings or years worked. In Georgia this has happened as a result of legislation; more typically it occurs as the result of minimum pension floors and maximum pension ceilings converging. Even more affluent countries, such as Latvia, went through periods of flattened pensions in the early 1990s before their economies started growing; others, such as Poland, have special regimes for the rural population that are essentially flat benefits.

Though poverty has increased in most of the region since the early 1990s, there is evidence indicating that pensioners were better protected than wage earners.[4] In less affluent and younger countries such as Albania or Turkmenistan, state pensions are buttressed by informal risk sharing mechanisms. In Georgia, for example, pensioners report that 15 percent of their income comes from private transfers. For some of the upper deciles, this is more than income from public pensions. In general, however, little is known about the role of informal intergenerational transfers in these countries.

Countries in the ECA region with the lowest replacement rates (as a share of income per capita) generally are the poorest in absolute terms. Under these circumstances, policymakers face a stark choice between policies of consumption

---

[3] E.g. Georgia raised retirement age by 5 years for men and women overnight.

[4] The income of pensioner households relative to dependent worker households increased during the transition in seven of the countries in his study (Czech Republic, Hungary, Latvia, Lithuania, Poland, Romania and Slovakia. The incidence of poverty among the old was lower than among all other age groups in Bulgaria, Belarus, Czech Republic, Hungary, Latvia, Poland and Russia. The converse was true only for Estonia. See Milanovic (1997).

smoothing (albeit with lower targets than in the past) or focusing their resources on poverty alleviation.

Once conditions permit -- ability to collect contributions, reliable state and private pension institutions -- the lower per capita income countries inevitably will move back toward greater differentiation in pension benefits, much as has occurred already in the higher income countries in the region. In those countries, such as Hungary and Poland, shifts in benefit formulas are underway to minimize re-distributions to lower income workers and more explicitly link benefits to contributions. This shift reflects both social norms about vertical equity and hopes that greater linkage will improve work and compliance incentives and, in so doing, help improve longer term financing.

As the ECA countries have considered their pension options, including the prospects of worsening system dependency ratios, they have had to think anew about the interactions of pensions, fiscal policy and economic growth, as well as social objectives. For some, this has meant adoption of a "multi-pillar model"[5]. These reforms shift a portion of the mandatory contribution to the pension system to private institutions that establish individual defined contribution accounts for each worker – often labeled as the "second pillar." An individual's eventual pension portfolio will consist of a benefit from a downsized "first pillar" public pension scheme (fully or mostly PAYG financed) plus a benefit purchased with accumulated funds from the second pillar.

Adoption of this model follows from several policy conclusions that are discussed at greater length in section two: individual accounts embody desirable work and compliance incentives; under the right fiscal conditions funding can increase a nation's savings and investment path overtime; funded accounts can accelerate a nation's capital market institutions and efficiency in capital allocation and, therefore, its economic growth rate; the returns on capital and labor differ over time and a multi-pillar systems thus allow individuals to diversify lifetime risks; and the funded component in a multi-pillar pension systems allows countries, especially smaller countries, to diversify their collective pension risks onto a larger economic base. Countries will design their second pillar components differently depending on which of these objectives are more paramount for each country.

In four countries in central and eastern Europe, reforms already have resulted in the introduction of second pillars. In Hungary, legislation passed in 1997 and was implemented in 1998. The result is that by 1999 2.1 million workers – mostly under age 40 and about 50 percent of the workforce – have diverted part of their pension contributions (6% of payroll) to private pension fund managers. All new labor market entrants are required to join. In 1999, workers in Poland between ages 30 and 50 were given the choice to divert one fifth of their overall pension contribution (7.2% of payroll) to newly licensed pension funds and their managers. Workers under 30 automatically joined the new scheme. More than 8 million people are now covered by the new multi-

---

[5] See Rutkowski (1998) for an overview of the movement towards multi-pillar systems in transition economies. For a more extensive discussion of the rational for a multi-pillar ("three pillar") model, see World Bank (1994), Averting the Old Age Crisis. For a review of recent developments in multi-pillar pension systems, see Fox and Palmer (November 1999 and June 2000).

pillar pension system in Poland. In Latvia, a smaller 2% of payroll pillar was introduced in 2000. In Croatia, a second pillar at 5% of payroll is set to begin on January 1, 2002.

In several countries, similar second pillars are being implemented or seriously considered. In Bulgaria and FYR Macedonia, the second pillar has been enacted in principle with actual introduction and size dependent of future fiscal conditions. Work on the second pillar concept proceeds in Estonia, Lithuania and Slovakia. In Romania, a working group has proposed that ten percentage points of the overall contribution should be diverted to private pensions, a proposal that is still being debated. Governments have announced plans to introduce initially small second pillars in Russia and Ukraine.

Introduction of a multi-pillar system with a mandatory funded component carries with it complex challenges, including some minimally sufficient conditions in terms of financial market development, as well as in administrative and supervisory capacities. In addition, a country must have a fiscally feasible strategy to deal with the diversion of revenues from a purely pay-as-you-go system to one with a funded component (usually labeled "transition costs"). The transition typically will impose welfare losses overtime that some countries are not prepared to legislate, and practical limits exist on how much of any shift to funding can be debt financed to match those losses overtime to economic gains. (For more discussion on this topic, see section three.) These constraints, however, should not prevent countries from improving both the adequacy and consumption smoothing aspects of their PAYG pension systems.

Some countries, such as Hungary, Croatia and Lithuania, have sought to improve the micro-economic aspects of their pension systems by improvements to traditional defined benefit formulas. Another, more fundamental, approach has been to re-characterize the ongoing PAYG promise in the terms of what occurs in a funded defined contribution account. This paradigm – often called a notional defined contribution (NDC) account or, more simply, a notional account – has proven effective in some countries in obtaining PAYG reform results that are resisted when advanced in the more traditional terms of parametric reform of defined benefit formulas. These reform results include use of lifetime wages for determining benefits, adjustments to reflect growing longevity and (possibly) declining fertility, and incentives for older workers to remain in the labor force and pay contributions.[6] As discussed below, pursing sound micro-economic incentives in pension policy has merits independent of funding.

---

[6] The prototype of notional account reforms in transition economies was Latvia, which followed the reform designed in Sweden. See Palmer (June 2000) for a discussion of the Swedish reform. Beginning with 1998 the Latvian pension system was converted into a new system based on individual accounts. Pension contributions are credited with an "interest rate" (that is, revalued) equal to growth in the country's aggregate wage; further, each person's pension depends on his or her accumulated amount divided up by the average life expectancy at the retirement age. The system therefore automatically adjusts to changes in the wage base and changes in life expectancy. Further, the system encourages working longer by using actuarially neutral factors to adjust for delays in drawing benefits and in giving credit for work after the first age of eligibility. For example, delaying retirement from age 62 or 63 and by working one year longer yields an 8-9% increase in the amount of pension, not the typical 2-3 % increase found in most traditional DB formulas in the region. See Fox and Palmer (August 1999) for more discussion of the Latvian reform.

The NDC or notional account approach was followed in Poland, where it was introduced on January 1, 1999 with respect to the PAYG components of the reform (which reform, as noted earlier, also includes a funded DC component). In addition, the notional account approach has attracted interest among CIS countries that are not yet in a position to think about multi-pillar systems. The Kyrgyz Republic introduced a notional account formula with respect to new accruals, and Moldova has the legislated objective to move toward use of a notional account formula in the future. The concept of notional accounts was considered carefully in Russia, and yet other countries, such as Azerbaijan, have expressed interest in examining it.

Reintroduction of more pronounced earnings-related elements in the pension systems of less affluent ECA countries poses a challenge for anti-poverty policies. The future distribution of pensions will resemble a growing distribution in wages, and the poverty rates in those countries are already high. On the other hand, the experience in most countries with mandatory pension systems is that, even if they start with a very anti-poverty and egalitarian orientation, they inevitably move toward some reflection of the differences in antecedent wage histories. As wage growth in lower per capita ECA countries begins to accelerate, pressures will mount to reintroduce differentiation, even retrospectively for those already retired. Countries will be challenged to find the right balance among maintaining a minimum pension at a level to minimize poverty among the aged and other pension populations, introduce earnings-related elements and contain overall pension spending within reasonable bounds. The earnings-related element might be some combination of the introduction of a funded second pillar for new accruals among younger workers with limited and complementary earnings-related PAYG elements – possibly along the lines of notional accounts – for transition cohorts. As discussed later, earnings-differentiation may be important in order to help induce labor market effects that are vital to the long term financing of pensions.

Table 1 below compares some of the key parameters of the reforms in five countries that have introduced or legislated a multi-pillar system. Only one non-European transition economy, Kazakhstan, has introduced a multi-pillar scheme. In addition to being an outlier in this sense, it is also distinct in that it has moved towards eventually a fully funded system, reducing the solidarity role to one of coping with the risks of poverty in old age or disability through means-testing.[7]

TABLE 1: FEATURES OF MULTI-PILLAR PROPOSALS IN SELECTED
TRANSITION ECONOMIES

	Starting Date	First pillar	Projected pension fund assets in 2020 (% GDP)	Workforce in funded pillar (2000)	Switching Strategy
Hungary	January 1998	PAYG DB	31%	45%	Mandatory new entrants Voluntary others

---

[7] In this regard, the Kazakh reform resembles the Chilean, El Salvadoran and Peruvian reforms in which no residual, pay-as-you go contributory scheme remained after the reform.

7

Poland	January 1999	NDC	33%	70%	Mandatory < 30, Voluntary 30-50
Kazakhstan	January 1998	Guaranteed minimum	30%	100%	Mandatory for all workers
Latvia	July 2001 (NDC January 1996)	NDC	20%	72%	Mandatory < 30, Voluntary 30-50
Croatia	January 2002	PAYG DB	25-30%	60-70%	Mandatory <40, Voluntary 40-50

Source: the authors, an expanded an updated version of the table in Palacios, Rutkowski, and Yu (1999)

2. The rationale for pension reforms

2.1 Labor market effects and the long-term balance of the pension systems

Pensions in the ECA region average at least 8% of ECA GDP and are largely financed by taxes on labor income. Reasonable baseline projections envisage that the pension burden will grow well above 14% of GDP within a few decades, or even above 16% of GDP with expected fertility and mortality changes. Such growth is likely to generate social and political unrest, and unless managed successfully, could undermine growth in employment, which, as seen below, is critical to a balanced solution.

In addition, ECA countries finance their pension expenditures by social security contributions at very high rates ranging from 20 percent to almost 40 percent on a comparable basis. These rates are a reflection of high system dependency ratios (beneficiaries over effective contributors). The adverse effect of high contribution rates on the labor market, especially detrimental effects on labor demand in the formal sector, should be a matter of serious concern of ECA policy makers. Accordingly, ECA countries face two simultaneous challenges for the sustainability of their pension systems: stabilization of pension expenditures *and* reduction in contribution rates.

To estimate the role of key factors that address these challenges, this section presents results of the analysis of a long-term balance of pension systems in a diverse sample of 9 ECA countries[8]. Though the analysis, presented in the appendix, is rather standard, it takes on board more explicitly than usual the labor market factors that can have an important effect on both the contribution rates and the long term fiscal balance of pension systems. Key variables are the labor force participation rate, the employment rate, the size of the formal labor market, and the degree of labor hoarding. Improvement

---

[8] The sample comprises 9 countries with 70% of the regional population. In the sample, there are 2 ECA countries with the largest population (Russia and Ukraine), 4 Central and Eastern European countries (Poland, Croatia, Lithuania and Estonia), 1 South-East European country (Moldova), 1 Caucasian country (Azerbaijan),and 1 Central Asian country (Kyrgyzstan).

in those variables can partially offset the negative trend with respect to the sustainability of PAYG pensions and contribution rates.

Our results are presented in Table 2. We first show what the current age profiles in the nine countries will do to pension spending without any changes in policy and without any improvements in either longevity or fertility (2050 projected expenditures). This alone will cause expenditures to increase from an average of 8.1 percent of GDP in 1997/98 (line 1) to 14.2 percent of GDP in 2050 (line 2).

We then estimate the additional effects of probable changes in mortality and fertility to the baseline scenario (2050 expenditures with mortality and fertility improvements). Under this adjusted mortality/fertility scenario, expenditures would be approximately 14 percent higher (line 3), increasing average pension expenditures to 16.5 percent of GDP (line 6). Either spending would have to be reduced by 51 percent (line 7) of the 16.5 percent of GDP, or revenues increased by an equivalent amount, to compensate.

Table 2: ECA pension systems long-term balance and labor market effects in percents of GDP										
	Azerbijan	Croatia	Estonia	Krygyz.	Lithuania	Moldova	Poland	Russia	Ukraine	Average
1. 1997-98 expenditures (%GPD)	3.3	9.8	9.7	6.5	6.1	7.4	14.2	6.9	9.3	8.1
2. 2050 projected expenditures (%GDP)	6.7	13.5	17.6	9.9	10.6	14.1	27.1	13.6	14.5	14.2
3. Combined demographic effects on 2050 expenditures, including:	2%	17%	11%	25%	5%	7%	26%	13%	22%	14%
4. mortality	11%	27%	26%	26%	17%	23%	23%	32%	37%	25%
5. fertility	-9%	-8%	-12%	-1%	-10%	-12%	3%	-14%	-11%	-8%
6. 2050 expenditures with demographic effects (% GDP)	6.8	15.9	19.4	12.3	11.1	15.3	34.5	15.5	17.6	16.5
7. Required compensating effect to stay at 97-98 expenditure level	-51%	-38%	-50%	-47%	-45%	-52%	-59%	-55%	-47%	-51%
8. Combined labor market effects, including:	-35%	-37%	-19%	-40%	-20%	-43%	-27%	-28%	-31%	-31%
9. LFP	-8%	-25%	-13%	-14%	-6%	-17%	-16%	-13%	-8%	-13%
10. Unemployment	-2%	-6%	-5%	-2%	-5%	-6%	-4%	-6%	-6%	-5%
11. FSP	-28%	-11%	-3%	-28%	-11%	-28%	-11%	-11%	-19%	-17%
12. Retirement age increase to 65/65	-38%	-33%	-30%	-42%	-33%	-37%	-15%	-32%	-34%	-32%
13. Real benefit relative to real wage growth										
14. 50 percent	-24%	-25%	-24%	-24%	-27%	-19%	-27%	-19%	-20%	-23%
15. 0 percent	-42%	-44%	-42%	-42%	-47%	-35%	-47%	-35%	-35%	-41%

Table 2 then outlines the effects of the various factors relative to line 6, that is, expenditures in 2050 with mortality and fertility improvements. Noteworthy is that increased revenues from the combined labor market effects (line 8) would go a long distance in filling the gap – about 60 percent of the average compensating gap. The least scope for optimism about potential contribution of improved labor markets is in the Baltic states of Lithuania and Estonia, where current LFP and/or FSP rates have stayed relatively high through the late 1990s.

Table 2 indicates that three main factors that can help in stabilizing pension expenditures by 2050 have roughly similar impacts: labor market effects at line 8, retirement age increases at line 12, and pension indexing (proxied by real benefit growth relative to productivity) at lines 14 and 15.[9] None of them alone can stabilize expenditures, however, two of the three together can do this.

Table 3 restates this analysis in terms of contribution rates. (The rates used here only include contributions to the pension scheme and have been adjusted across countries to have the uniform *legal* incidence that the entire contribution falls on the employer.) The last line indicates that the countries in the region cannot count on labor market effects alone to contain contribution rates at the 1997-98 levels, which levels are in some countries are already very high. Some combination of retirement age increases and reduction in average benefit levels will be necessary to contain and, preferably, lower contribution rates.

Table 3: ECA pension systems long-term balance and labor market effects in contribution rates on employers

	Azerbaijan	Croatia	Estonia	Kyrgyzstan	Lithuania	Moldova	Poland	Russia	Ukraine	Average
1997-98 rates	32.0	24.1	20.0	36.4	23.7	28.8	38.8	29.3	33.3	29.6
2050 equivalent rates	65	33	36	55	41	55	74	58	52	52
2050 with mortality and fertility effects	66	39	40	69	43	59	93	65	63	59
2050 with labor markets only	42	21	29	33	33	31	54	42	36	36
2050 with demographic and labor effects	43	24	33	42	35	33	68	47	44	41

Though the three factors – labor market changes, retirement age increases and lowering average benefits through less generous indexing rules -- have similar impact on pension expenditures, their effects on holding down the contribution rates could be different. Raising retirement ages – that is, raising the ages at which benefits can first be drawn – reinforces the labor market effects. Our analysis captures some of this effect. Prior the transition shocks of the early 90s, older workers did not always retire when first eligible. Returning to 1990s labor force participation levels implies an increase in work among older workers (relative to those levels in the late 1990s), as well as an increase among women's labor force participation at many ages. An increase in formal retirement ages would help return older workers' labor force participation to previous levels, thus helping reduce the numerator (benefiticiaries) and the denominator (contributors) in the system dependency ratio.

In contrast, even if it were possible through pension indexating rules or other means, to downscale average benefits enough to keep pension expenditures at 1997-98

---

[9] Less than full wage indexing of benefits in pay status can have a significant effect on pension spending as a percent of either GDP or payroll. The effect, however, is very sensitive to assumptions about productivity growth. If benefits are adjusted by inflation plus 50 percent of real wage growth, the ratio of real average pension to real average wage will drop over fifty years by 25 percent if average productivity is only 1 percent per year, and by 50 percent if average productivity is as much as 3 percent per annum. It should be kept in mind, however, that real benefit levels (purchasing power) are much higher in a world of 3 percent per annum productivity growth. Ratio declines are even more dramatic (40 and 70 percent, respectively) if benefits are adjusted to price growth alone. In a world of continually high productivity, a country likely would opt for higher lifetime replacement rates. As discussed in section three, for the same level of spending over an extended period, this can mean either higher initial replacement rates and less generous indexing, or it can mean lower initial replacement rates and more generous indexing.

levels, the effects on contribution rates are not so obvious. Spending might be kept down to levels that vitiated further increases in contribution rates, but it is unlikely that contribution rates could be lowered from today's already high levels. And, the lower those rates, the more likely that the society will realize the labor force effects in these projections.

Our analysis suggests two broad conclusions. The first is that microeconomic incentives encouraging labor market participation and employment will play an important role in re-balancing mandatory pension systems. The second is that in order to achieve both the stabilization of pension expenditures *and* the reduction in contribution rates, it is essential to focus on factors that improve the system dependency ratio, that is, retirement age increases, reduction in unemployment, improved labor forced participation, and reduction in the share of the informal economy that does not contribute to the pension system.

In terms of policy implications, our analysis emphasizes that although pension policy is but one tool in changing those labor market incentives, careful attention should be paid in pension redesigns to encouraging long term labor force participation with clear rewards at the margin for paying contributions, especially at older ages. The notional account paradigm may be a helpful concept to effect those changes. Even where it is not used, the concept is a useful anchor in helping specify parametric changes in more conventional DB formulas (e.g., for setting the value of credit for delayed retirement or the decrement for early retirement).[10] Incentives, however, need to be buttressed with modernization of collection and compliance mechanisms.

2.2 A multi-pillar pension system

In order to improve microeconomic labor market incentives, in addition to expected macroeconomic effects, an increasing number of ECA countries have replaced the PAYG monopoly by a multi-pillar system that consists of a PAYG pillar and a funded pillar. The logic behind is as follows. Both pillars have risks, and not all the risks are the same. A partial switch would allow workers to *diversify risks* better. They would face a multi-pillar mandatory system and they would achieve returns based on different kinds of assets in each pillar. In the case of the public PAYG schemes (conventional DB or notional account), the return depends on the growth of wages. In the case of the new private scheme, it depends on returns to capital. As long as these two are not correlated, some diversification gain is possible. Limited empirical evidence for OECD countries suggests that the correlation between the two is low or non-existent, supporting the diversification argument.[11] Moreover, having experienced first hand the political or policy risks inherent

---

[10] It is also important for coverage of pension systems. Making formal retirement system portable, transparent and flexible is an important condition for maintaining or achieving high coverage. See Holzmann, Packard and Cuesta (January 2000).

[11] Correlation coefficients for long time series of wage growth and equity returns were not found to be significantly different than zero in the Netherlands, US, UK, Japan and Germany. Palacios (December 1998) and Thompson (1998), Appendix Table A. This lack of correlation within countries between wage and capital growth may be less applicable to transition and developing economies. See discussion below concerning diversification across countries.

in the public pension schemes, workers were receptive to the idea of spreading their risks between public and private sector institutions.[12]

Certainly, the difference between PAYG and funding should not overshadow consideration of other policy choices in pension design that may be as important (Barr 2000). Funding is only one element in a large policy mix that includes also issues like minimum pensions, demogrants, means testing, different types of management of pension assets, as well as the microeconomic incentives discussed earlier.

In Figure 1, the first pillar is mandatory and PAYG, the second pillar is mandatory and funded, and third pillar is voluntary and funded. The third pillar serves the needs of those who wish to retire earlier or have living standards in retirement that exceed those likely to occur from required social security contributions. Figure 1 portrays the dual

**Figure 1: A Multi-pillar Pension System
and Role of Second Pillar**

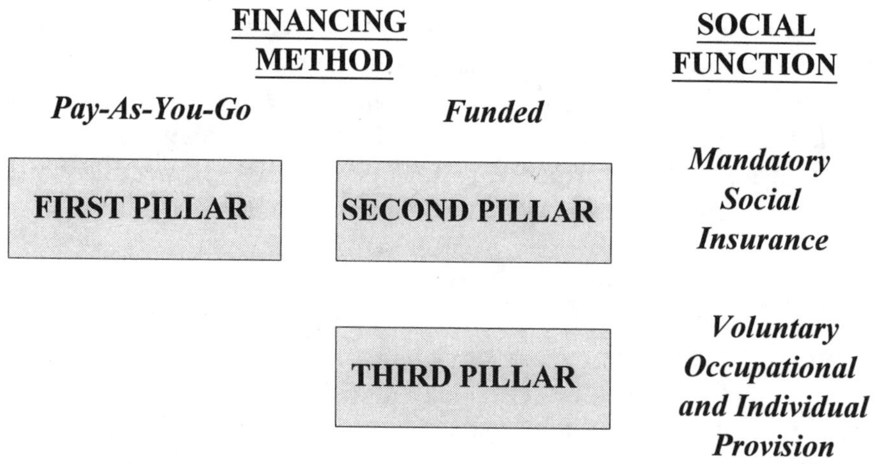

FINANCING METHOD		SOCIAL FUNCTION
Pay-As-You-Go	*Funded*	
FIRST PILLAR	**SECOND PILLAR**	*Mandatory Social Insurance*
	THIRD PILLAR	*Voluntary Occupational and Individual Provision*

Source: Gora and Rutkowski (1998)

nature of the second pillar. From a financing perspective, the second and third pillars are funded. From a functional perspective, the first and second pillars are mandatory and financed within a unitary social security contribution rate. Though it has more aspects of private property than usually attributed to PAYG pensions, the second pillar, nonetheless, is part of an overall social security system where societal objectives are at least equally as important as norms of individual equity and standard notions of private property.

Moving to a multi-pillar arrangement also responds to economic goals: by creating a *mandatory pension that is invested in the capital markets,* a country's *growth path is potentially increased* by reason of more efficient capital allocation and, less clearly,

---

[12] This argument was used effectively in the Polish reform effort under the label "Security through Diversity". See Government of Poland (June 1997), Gora and Rutkowski (1998), and Chlon, Gora, and Rutkowski (August 1999).

higher savings and investment. In addition, introduction of a funded pillar also introduces the potential for *international diversification.* To the extent that aggregate shocks affect a certain country or even a region, investing abroad can provide the same or greater return with less risk. While the correlation between returns in rich country capital markets has been increasing, significant gains are still possible, especially in developing countries.[13]

Introduction of multi-pillar pension systems is likely to increase the workers' sense of *individual responsibility* about their future retirement. This occurs because most second pillar designs give workers responsibility for choosing which investment manager will manage the investment of their second pillar contributions. This sense of individual responsibility is buttressed if the costs of the full system are made *more transparent* by a concurrent shift of a share of today's payroll tax in the amount of the second pillar contribution (along with a "gross up" in workers' wages). This second step can be taken independently of the introduction of a second pillar.

Multi-pillar pension systems also may mitigate political pressures on the retirement system by *diversifying retirement risks* across the political and financial spheres. By diversifying the financing of the retirement system, ECA countries can accomplish the goal of maintaining a level close to today's replacement rates at a lower and politically *more sustainable contribution rate* than would be the case in a pure pay-as-you-go retirement system. This objective, however, can be achieved only by a shifting of costs to other revenue sources or contractions in pension or other spending. These welfare losses, however, are offset if the introduction of a funded pension boosts the country's further GDP through increased national savings in the intermediate term and/or significant increase of the depth and liquidity of capital markets. These gains may be particularly important among younger workers, allowing them to share in what is a one-off increase in a transition economy's return on capital.

Maintaining appropriate *adequacy target* in the mandatory pension system is an important binding constraint. With the introduction of the second pillar, further reductions of the first pillar should focus on raising the effective retirement age and ensuring adequate protection for the poor by minimum pensions and other mechanisms.

Achieving these objectives of a multi-pillar reform requires careful design of the funded pillar, including determining its size and financing options, and establishing its institutional framework. Furthermore, it is important to adjust the first pillar to clearly define its role and structure. The goal of strengthening individual responsibility, transparency and political insulation can be seriously compromised unless some regular and reasonably predictable valorization and indexing standards are introduced into the first pillar. Shifting more of the apparent contribution burden to workers, including a portion of the contribution that is used to finance first pillar would also increase the awareness of individuals regarding the cost of state pensions. The next section discusses these design issues in greater detail.

---

[13] See Holzmann (2000) for simulated risk reduction effects. Also see Holzmann (May 2000) on the extent to which investment in emerging markets can reduce retirement age and other adjustments in developed countries.

The question is sometimes asked why ECA countries do not move more aggressively towards the "fully funded" model of, for example, Chile and other (but not all) Latin American countries. Without getting into the debate about the merits of the full switch option, it is important to highlight here that transition costs play a major limiting role in the ECA region. Most ECA countries have large levels of implicit pension debt, quite settled expectations about retirement ages and replacement rates, and economies that still are undergoing the difficult process of becoming fully market-based. As discussed immediately below, in each country there exist financial and distributional (political) limits on increasing a country's explicit debt to smooth out transition costs. Any country with a large level of antecedent PAYG coverage would have difficulty in convincing long-term lenders (including its own citizens) that over some very extended period, transcending elections and supervening economic events, it could manage a rapid build-up and then gradual retirement of external debt equal to its entire implicit pension debt. Accordingly, the challenge in the ECA region has been to find a balance that recognizes these constraints while still shifting enough to a funded component to achieve needed economic growth effects (particularly those associated with the development of and more effective operation of capital markets).

3. Dilemmas and emerging solutions with respect to reforms and reformed systems

In this section of our paper, we discuss some of the experiences of, and choices made by, countries that have begun implementing multi-pillar pension systems with a funded second pillar or that are relatively advanced in the planning process.[14] Not all that has occurred has been without problems so there are lessons to be learned from these prior experiences, as well as how fiscal constraints and social norms have shaped them. The area is somewhat new. Though experts in the field occasionally will express strong views about what a reforming country should do with respect to one design element or another, the reality is that there are no clear "best" practices, but rather choices among what might be termed "good" alternatives.

3.1 Size of the second pillar and financing the transition

Size of the second pillar. The preferred size of any mandatory funded second pillar (measured as percentage points of payroll or GDP going to finance it) is inevitably influenced by what are the objectives or expected benefits from the pension reform, and the economic and institutional constraints on achieving these objectives. In determining the scale of the funded pillar and the financing of transition, governments need to take a comprehensive approach and understand various tradeoffs based on careful analysis of the economic and social effects.

---

[14] We do not cover in this paper the entire range of second pillar design issues with which countries must grapple. For example, we do not discuss the options for how PAYG, second pillar pensions, or voluntary retirement savings (third pillar) might be handled in a country's business and household tax regimes. In this regard, care must be taken so that the second pillar receives no less favorable tax treatment than that afforded the PAYG pillar. A larger pension reform also may offer the occasion to rationalize existing tax policies toward retirement and other savings. For a discussion of alternative tax treatments for retirement, see Whitehouse (June 1999).

When starting to consider introducing a second pillar, it helps to specify some initial bounds on the feasible sizes of any funded pillar between which choice can be made based on further economic analysis and international experience. In this respect, based on what has occurred in terms of institutional arrangements in most countries, it is doubtful if a second pillar of less than 4-6% of payroll would be cost effective.

This lower bound exists because policy-makers are faced with two objectives that are not easy to reconcile in practice. The first is that assets going into a second pillar arrangement must be invested according to market signals if the conversion to funding is to contribute to future economic growth. This requires insulation from political influence as to where the moneys are invested, except as reflected in transparent and prudential regulations (discussed later). In some political economies, it may be possible to design governance procedures for funded account schemes or reserve/buffer funds in state DB or NDC systems (which also depend on PAYG financing) that both keep transaction costs very low through centralized asset management and still assure that investment choice is insulated from inappropriate political influence.[15] In recent years, however, many countries have determined that effective insulation from political interference in pension asset management requires giving workers choice among competing fund managers, as well as other indicia of ownership. So far, worker-choice second pillars have entailed *pro rata* fixed costs that caution against going below 4-6 % of payroll. Ongoing work in Sweden and elsewhere may yield results in the next few year that demonstrate the feasibility of worker-choice second pillars in the range of 2-3% of payroll.[16]

The constraints on the maximum size of the second pillar are more complex.[17] Experience in the region suggests that analysis should begin with an upper bound on the contribution rate for the second pillar in the range of 7-10% of payroll. With the exception of Kazakhstan, ECA countries that adopted a mandatory funded pension scheme also decided to retain an explicit permanent (downsized) PAYG first pillar and a (larger) PAYG-only option for older workers. Accordingly, a large fraction of any existing contribution rate must be reserved for PAYG financing. As discussed further below, transitions to second pillars are often financed from "within" the existing pension system by changes in formulas and indexing rules and in retirement ages, all of which changes have socially and, therefore, politically tolerable limits. Some debt and tax financing from outside the antecedent pension system typically augments transition financing, but here too competing social and economic considerations impose limits. In

---

[15] See chapter five of Herbertsson, Orzag and Orzag (May 2000) for discussion of insulated centrally managed schemes in Nordic countries. For a discussion of the largely poor track record of state management of either individual account schemes ("Provident Funds") and reserve or buffer funds in partially funded state pension schemes, see Palacios and Iglesias (January 2000).

[16] The Swedish scheme, though very open ended in terms of worker choice among investment alternatives, depends heavily on a state-managed collection and clearinghouse system and places severe limits on the interactions of fund managers with clients. As discussed later, these are preconditions that are not easy to establish. Geographical and population size also may affect preconditions. What might be feasible and cost effective in Latvia or Sweden might not work as well in Romania, Poland or the United States.

[17] For a short overview of this topic, see Chapter 8 in Thompson (1998). For an extensive discussion of measuring implicit pension liabilities, options for managing their full or partial conversion to explicit liabilities and other matters related to financing the transition, see Holzmann (December 1998). See Brooks and James (September 1999) for more discussion of the size of countries' implicit pension debt and the capacity and willingness to move toward funding.

light of the inherited target replacement and contribution rates prevalent in the region, all these various constraints have made 7-10% of payroll the conventional upper bound on second pillars in the ECA region. Macroeconomic limitations have tended to constrain the maximum towards the lower end of this range.

Another key element dictating the size of the second pillar – particularly during the initial years after its introduction – are the rules adopted about who (if any) shall be covered on a mandatory basis, who (if any) should be excluded, and the incentives offered to those whose participation in the second pillar is elective. Normative and prudential concerns, as well as transition costs determine choices about coverage, which issues are discussed later.

Concerns over transition costs have led some countries to consider phasing-in the second pillar; that is, start at some quite low level, such as two percent, and then increase the second pillar contribution rate over some period (such as 10-20 years) to a level in the 7-10 percent range. While appealing at first blush, this approach complicates most all other design considerations and makes the second pillar's onset and ultimate size subject to changing political economy factors. For example, in Hungary a new government in 1997, unsympathetic to the pension reform enacted under the prior one, postponed further increases in the second pillar percentage. This change in policy disrupted both the expectations of workers who joined the second pillar assuming the higher levels and the business plans of fund managers. On balance, a one-step reform appears preferable, especially since roughly comparable inter-temporal cost sharing can be achieved through use of some debt financing. In addition, the phase-in strategy delays the economic benefits from capital market development.

Financing the transition. While the long-run benefits of any well-designed pension reform should outweigh long-run costs, the shift to a funded system almost always requires additional resources beyond those needed to service existing state pension commitments. Either the overall contribution rate must be raised to accommodate an added second pillar, or moneys previously used to finance ongoing PAYG spending are diverted to the funded pillar to purchase financial assets, leaving a fiscal hole in the PAYG system. This is often labeled the "double pay" problem.

Debt financing. In thinking about the challenges and options involved with moving toward to a pension regime that contains a funded component, a useful concept to employ is "implicit pension debt." Existing pension PAYG promises are like formal government bonds, although typically much more conditional.[18] In theory, each country's fiscal balance sheet reflects not only its explicit or formal debt, but also its implicit debt for PAYG pensions and similar promises. If financial markets viewed each kind of debt as perfectly equivalent, a country could swap implicit for explicit debt with impunity. That is, the government could finance transition costs by borrowing either domestically

---

[18] How conditional may depend to some degree on how a country's high court interprets provisions of its organic law (constitution) concerning property rights (including possibly accrued rights from state schemes) and strictures against unfair procedures or classifications. Constitutions themselves may contain very detailed and directive provisions. And, of course, the interplay of political forces always places limits on how much a PAYG promise can be changed or truncated under different economic conditions.

or overseas to pay for ongoing PAYG promises, freeing up equivalent amounts in new pension contributions for workers to purchase second pillar financial assets. Hypothetically, this *debt financing* might equal the full amount of the second pillar contribution rate until such time that ongoing PAYG spending could be solely financed by the contribution rate permanently assigned to the first pillar.

Debt financing, however, is not a costless shift in financing. Holding all else equal, the extra borrowing and explicit debt carries with it an equally explicit ongoing cost -- higher annual debt service. This higher interest amount must be mostly offset by decreased government spending elsewhere or by higher taxes. The nonsustainable alternative would be ever increasing spiral of borrowing to pay ever-higher interest amounts as well as new increments of annual transition costs.

In this sense, debt financing necessarily carries with it some companion *tax financing*, a term of art that in this context connotes not just literally higher taxes but also less government spending.[19] The need to raise other taxes (e.g., income or VAT taxes) or reduce other government spending to compensate for the higher interest amount will impose limit on how much a country chooses to debt finance a transition. Other aspects of tax financing are discussed more extensively below.

In addition, financial markets know that most countries' implicit pension debts are very conditional. Lenders may react negatively if a country overreaches in swapping too much explicit debt for implicit debt, the latter of which is generally regarded as having higher default probabilities (that is, countries do restructure PAYG promises in light of ongoing and projected revenue limits). The tipping point will differ among countries according to their already accumulated explicit debt, recent trends in debt levels, the credibility of macroeconomic and fiscal policies and the country's basic endowments.

In addition, ECA countries that aspire to European Union accession face the debt and deficit limits embodied in the Maastricht treaty – that a country's total explicit debt not exceed 60 percent of GDP and annual deficits should not exclude 3 percent. For countries approaching the 60 percent debt limit, little room is left for debt financing the transition to funded pensions. Even for those well below the limit, they have to balance other possible uses of debt against pension transition costs.

Despite these fiscal, legal and macro-economic limits, debt financing remains a means, an almost inescapable means[20], by which countries can spread the higher up-front

---

[19] It can be argued that, in countries that chose to finance all or some of the switch from PAYG to funding by adding to their explicit debt, the extra interest traceable to those higher amounts of explicit debt is only making explicit an antecedent "tax" in the PAYG system. Most mature PAYG systems have internal rates of return that fall below rates of return on capital – a difference that can be viewed as a hidden tax. Putting to the side any growth effects from a switch to funding, the wedge between the PAYG and capital rates of return equals the extra interest on explicit debt incurred in converting implicit pension debt to funding. See Geanakoplos, Mitchell and Zeldes (1998) for a full discussion of this equivalence in the U.S. context. Though prior generations received welfare "windfalls" that equal the subsequent PAYG "tax," some of those gains may be passed down to later generations through intra-household transfers, directly or indirectly (e.g., higher investment in education). See also Disney (August 1999) for a fuller discussion of the "Aaron-Samuelson" condition and PAYG vs. funded rates of return.

[20] The alternative is a very slow phase-in of the second pillar, which carries with it the practical and

costs of transition over a longer period. The initial diversion of resources to the second pillar will be broadly proportional to its size and how much assessable wages are as a percent of GDP. In most ECA countries, a second pillar financed by a contribution rate of 8% of gross wage would require resources equal to around 2.5% to 3.2% of GDP during the initial years of reform if all workers were covered. Even if initial participation were constrained to only 50 to 60 percent of the covered workforce, the resources needed would be 1.25 to 1.9 percent of GDP. As noted below, amounts of this magnitude cannot be covered in the initial years by sufficiently large offsetting adjustments in the PAYG pension system. Further, most finance ministers likely would find it difficult to make immediate modifications in this magnitude to other government spending and taxation. Some debt financing allows these adjustments to be elongated and managed.

A particularly attractive form of debt financing in countries moving from state socialism to private ownership is to dedicate *privatization receipts* from the sale of formerly owned state enterprises to finance transition costs.[21] By this means, the government limits the amount of explicit debt it must incur (by selling an existing asset) and, in so doing, coincidentally helps create a stock of capital assets that can be purchased by the newly started second pillar funds.[22] This helps jumpstart the more efficient allocation of existing capital that can help raise a country's growth rate.

Even when debt financing takes the form of explicit government debt, rather than the sale of (now) non-government assets, the creation of a domestic capital market in government debt, where a market previously did not exist, can be beneficial. The existence of relatively liquid government bonds provides a useful benchmark for efficiently pricing private sector debt, and thereby helps deepen capital market development.

Tax Financing. Reforming countries also may have recourse to the following measures to finance the transition, all of which can be considered a form of tax financing.

Subvention from the Budget. In theory, a government's central Budget could finance a portion of the transition costs (over and beyond that which might be necessary to offset higher interest payments from debt financing). Given already high tax burdens and expenditure demands from all other quarters, the usual policy conclusion is that the pension reform has to be largely self-financing. In Poland, however, the need to deal with transition financing has put added emphasis of paring down the Budget to the essential core functions of the state, a reduction in subsidies to large state enterprises and utilities. Governments also might consider special purpose tax diversions or increases

---

political economy risks discussed earlier.

[21] A variation on this theme is to run down the reserves in the pre-reform pension system. A number of countries have "partial reserve" pension system that rely on a combination of (mostly) ongoing PAYG financing and investment returns from a stock of assets created built up during the system's initial years. Sweden had such a system and has decided to move to one with smaller first pillar promises, a lower level of first pillar reserves, and a new explicit second pillar. In effect, as the size of the first pillar buffer fund is reduced, money is moved into second pillar accounts. This makes the transition relatively easy.

[22] All other things being equal, however, use of privatization proceeds also means higher ongoing interest payments. The proceeds could have been used to pay down existing public debt, thereby lowering ongoing financing costs.

from, e.g., "sin" taxes, that might be politically sellable, particularly to mitigate the speed at which first pillar adjustments otherwise would have to occur.

Increased pension contribution rate. A country might choose to finance some or all of the costs of a second pillar by raising the overall contribution rate. With few exceptions, the overall tax burden, including contributions for pensions and other social insurance, is high in the ECA countries, a situation that has led to informalization and other forms of noncompliance. Thus, the starting presumption in most deliberations about introducing a second pillar is that its eventual cost has to be squeezed within the contribution rate that currently .exists. In some instances, this constraint may have to give somewhat to allow a successful reform to occur.

A seemingly less painless increase in contributions is that which may come overtime from greater compliance. Reform of the pension system, including the introduction of a second pillar, may improve compliance, as we discussed earlier in section two. Greater management and resource attention to the machinery of collection and compliance may also help. Governments also can take other steps to increase the economic advantages of "formalization," such that the economic benefits of being in the formal economy outweigh the advantages of tax noncompliance. Most long-term modeling assumes that over extended periods, compliance in the ECA region will rebound, at least in terms of wage reporting among whom the state can reach in the formal sector. As we saw from section two, however, gains from greater *formal* labor force participation and compliance are central to any strategy to simply balance existing PAYG promises. Accordingly, unless gains from increased compliance exceed what is needed to help balance PAYG commitments, better compliance – even back to the pre-transition levels we simulate in section two – does not fill the second pillar transition gap by itself.

It is worth noting, however, that increased formalization and compliance will also increase other revenues, such as income taxes. Holding all other spending constant, some of those moneys might be used to help finance the second pillar transition costs, though at the cost of otherwise lower tax rates.

Further limiting first pillar expenditures. As we observed in section two, some adjustments in first pillar benefit levels (replacement rates at retirement, post-retirement indexing, and retirement ages) will be necessary just to bring first pillar spending into balance, along with hoped for increases in labor force participation and compliance. These are policy adjustments that would have to occur even if there is no second pillar. In figure two, this is difference, shown as A, between the ovals of "existing PAYG promises" and "balanced PAYG promises."

In addition, unless the second pillar is designed to be completely additive to an otherwise balanced first pillar[23], some adjustment will be made to downsize first pillar accruals in conjunction with accruals in the second pillar. These reductions relate to first

---

[23] Part of the ongoing debate in Lithuania, where benefit levels are low relative to higher per capita countries such as Poland and Hungary, is whether a second pillar should be additive or an eventual substitute for an existing PAYG earning-related second tier.

pillar rights that do not mature for two or more decades. Because second pillar accumulations are designed to match these first pillar reductions, there are no significant welfare loses imposed. In figure 2, this is the difference, shown as B, between the ovals of "balanced PAYG promises" and "balanced PAYG with 2nd pillar offset." In terms of the practical politics of pension reform, it is often difficult to achieve the reductions necessary to bring PAYG liabilities in line with projected resources (the "A" area). Introducing a second pillar, along with the additional adjustments denoted in the "B" area, can create a political dynamic that makes overall PAYG downsizing easier to achieve. The appeal of funding to younger generations was a key ingredient in building the coalition necessary in Hungary and Poland to downsize the long term PAYG promises to more manageable levels.

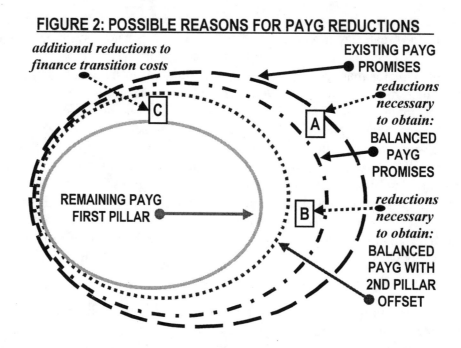

FIGURE 2: POSSIBLE REASONS FOR PAYG REDUCTIONS

additional reductions to finance transition costs

EXISTING PAYG PROMISES

reductions necessary to obtain:

BALANCED PAYG PROMISES

reductions necessary to obtain:

BALANCED PAYG WITH 2ND PILLAR OFFSET

C

A

B

REMAINING PAYG FIRST PILLAR

Typically, however, first pillar reductions in multi-pillar reforms have been deeper than that necessary to balance first pillar expenditures alone (with no second pillar) or to only offset future second pillar benefits. In effect, some of the transition burden is borne by retirees and older workers -- usually in the form of higher retirement ages and less generous post-retirement indexing. In general, such reductions in future first pillar spending are labeled tax financing,[24] but they might equally be viewed as reducing the starting amount of the country's implicit pension debt and, hence, a means of debt financing. In figure 2, this difference, shown as C, between the ovals of "balanced PAYG with 2nd pillar offset" and "remaining first pillar."[25]

---

[24] Palacios and Rocha (April 1998) for example.

[25] As discussed in the next section, there may be welfare gains from greater economic growth that offset these losses not just to future generations but also to older workers and younger retirees.

20

Balancing the transition costs. Placing the entire burden of transition on any single source is likely to be sub-optimal. First, full reliance on cutting first pillar expenditures could cut average replacement rates to unacceptably low levels, especially in the early and middle years of the transition, and any increase in retirement ages usually take place gradually over decades to allow workers and labor markets to adjust. Second, excessive reliance on deficit financing could lead to a rapid accumulation of government debt and increase in macroeconomic risks. Finally, reliance on tax increases could lead to excessively sharp short-term rises in the burden of taxes and contributions, further distorting labor markets and compliance and shifting too much of the cost of reform to younger generations.

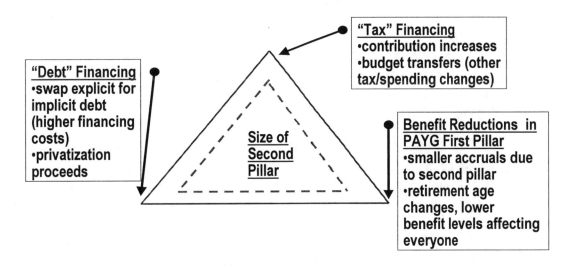

It is important to carefully consider the size and distribution of all benefits, costs and risks when deciding on the size and financing of the second pillar. In some instances, based on very preliminary analysis, policy-makers stipulate a second pillar target at the high end of the range (for example, based on many Latin American countries, 10 percent). As subsequent analysis makes the costs or risks of transition to a second pillar to that size more evident, policy-makers then shift to considering smaller second pillars, with both commensurately smaller risks and smaller potential benefits.

The divisions between debt and tax financing are somewhat arbitrary and tend to understate the key role of the pension system's implicit debt at the outset of the reform. Accordingly, as illustrated in figure 3, it may be useful to think of the trade-offs as occurring on three points of a triangle.[26] Each point entails some welfare losses.

---

[26] Credit for first designing a triangle along these lines to illustrate these transition trade-offs goes to Ardo Hansson, World Bank economist.

The other dimension is illustrated by the size of the triangular figure itself. The smaller the triangle, the smaller the transition cost challenge, the less painful the trade-offs that have to be made. Commensurately, of course, the smaller the economic gains from the second pillar, which also have their welfare gains. What is not being captured in this figure (and in much of the modeling) are the welfare gains that accrue to all the generations, including the retired and older workers, from increased economic growth traceable to a more funded pension system: greater labor force participation and compliance, more efficient capital allocation and possibly greater savings and investment. Unfortunately, it more even difficult to forecast and quantify these gains at the individual level in way comparable to how benefit losses and contribution increases can be forecast and quantified.

- At one point in the triangle are the options to reduce total implicit pension debt (benefit reductions) along the lines outlined in figure two. This can entail welfare losses to retirees and older workers. In the longer run, second pillar benefits will compensate younger workers for much of their losses in the first pillar, although they are likely to face higher retirement ages.

- At another point are the traditional debt financing options. These include use of privatization resources and converting some of the implicit pension debt into explicit debt. Either entails higher financing costs; who bears the associated welfare losses depends on how the impact of that extra burden is allocated within the nation's overall budget.

- At the third point are the traditional tax financing options. These include contribution increases and a shift to other revenue sources. Contribution increases are borne by workers and employers; the welfare losses associated with a shift to other revenue sources depends again on how the consequences are allocated within the nation's overall budget.

3. 2. Participation requirement in the new system

Determining the participation requirements for any multi-pillar system involves intersecting decisions about values concerning choice and protecting individuals from unwise choices, transition cost considerations and the virtue of keeping the reform as simple as possible.

Multi-pillar schemes typically are designed so that replacement rates (though not typically retirement ages) are relatively constant across generations. But defined benefit and defined contribution schemes have different accrual patterns. For those within 10 to 15 years of retirement, standard individual capitalized accounts are unlikely to generate an amount equal to what an individual would lose by moving a downsized PAYG scheme (that is, one with smaller accruals at the margin that recognize the introduction at the margin of a new second pillar). Accordingly, multi-pillar pension reforms in the region have had to create PAYG-only cognates to protect those for whom switching to a multi-pillar system would be injurious. In addition, individuals have different risk-reward preferences. Many younger workers, unschooled in capital markets, would prefer to stay entirely in a state wage based regime.

These just outlined considerations are often overlaid with political and sometimes legal needs to recognize the settled expectations of older workers. As a result, the policies concerning coverage in a multi-pillar scheme can become quite complicated.

- In Poland, though the reform laws were generally effective January 1999, an inherited PAYG regime (old law) was retained for cohorts born before 1949 (those over age 50 in 1999). This regime included special early retirement rights ("privileges") that enjoyed both legal and intense political protection. On the whole, it was easier to simply preserve old law PAYG for older workers than design complicated accrued rights in the successor PAYG regime for them. For those born between 1949 and 1968 (those 31 through age 50 in 1999), a choice exists between (a) remaining in a new law PAYG-only scheme (that uses notional account logic) or (b) switching to a multi-pillar system with a PAYG first pillar (a smaller version of the PAYG-only notional account scheme) and a funded DC second pillar.[27] Those age 30 or younger, as well as new entrants, have no choice and are covered only in the multi-pillar system.

- In Hungary, January 1998 was the effective date for both a reformed ("modernized") PAYG-only regime and a multi-pillar system that contains a downsized version of the modernized PAYG-only regime and a funded DC second pillar. The provisions of the PAYG reform law gradually changes both PAYG components overtime. Legal limits on accrued rights required that election between the two options was open to all workers regardless of age. Only new entrants to the labor force were required to enroll in the multi-pillar option. Accordingly, incentives were created within the two options to encourage older workers to choose the PAYG-only option and younger workers to choose the multi-pillar option.[28] The government also mounted an extensive public information campaign to encourage the public to make informed and rational choices.

Other countries in the course of implementing multi-pillar systems have developed their own variations. For example, in Croatia and Latvia, reform proceeded in two steps. The inherited PAYG system was first reformed: in Latvia by using the notional account paradigm, in Croatia by freely adapting aspects of the 1991 German law. In both instances, this first stage of transition contained provisions to recognize accrued rights and prevent any sharp discontinuities from one cohort to another. In the second stage, individuals will either remain in the reformed PAYG system or move to the multi-pillar alternative in which, at the margin, accruals in that PAYG system are reduced and funded second pillar accounts are introduced. Each country has its own mix of compulsion and choice with respect to age (see Table one).

The experience in Hungary and Poland is that most workers between the lower age bound (entry or age 30) and the age of 50 have chosen to enroll in the multi-pillar option.

---

[27] For details about the Polish reform, see Chlon, Gora and Rutkowski (August 1999).
[28] For details about the Hungarian reform, see Palacios and Rocha (April 1998).

The fact that most chose to join the new system was seen as a broad public affirmation for and acceptance of the reform, and makes it less likely to be reversed by subsequent governments.

In addition, making choice available to a larger segment of the work force reduces transition costs (and complexity of transition provisions) compared to scenarios in which everyone is required to join the multi-pillar new system. This can lead, however, to higher uncertainty in estimating he transaction cost. Each country has to weigh the potential political advantage of allowing a broad segment of the population to make an affirmative decision ratifying the reform against the added uncertainty in estimating the transition costs. Allowing choice also carries the obligation that the government conduct effective communication with the public to assist individuals in making informed switching decisions.[29]

3.3 Adjusting the first pillar

Creating a stable two-pillar pension system often requires a more predictable and transparent first pillar pension (and, often, an alternative PAYG mono-pillar). Workers can hardly be expected to assume more responsibility for their own retirement planning if the key components of the first pillar pension are adjusted each year through an opaque and unpredictable political process. Unless the pre-existing system is very small and the second pillar purely additive, the reform should include both a redesign of the first pillar to take into account the benefits to be provided by the new second pillar and the adoption of adjustment rules that, though they can be altered in the face of temporary economic difficulties, provides a degree of predictability to future benefits.

Adjusting benefit formulas. Usually the benefit level must be adjusted in light of the introduction of the second pillar. This can raise a host of distributional issues concerning those with low lifetime earnings, the treatment of women, credit for schooling and periods of unemployment, and so on. In theory all these social concerns could pertain equally to funded second pillars, but because funded accounts are typically characterized as having attributes of private property, the first pillar typically bears the brunt of such concerns. An exhaustive discussion of this matter goes beyond the bounds of this paper, but one tendency is worth noting; formula reforms that retain overt redistribution appear not to enjoy any broad public support in the region.

The early round of reforms in the early 1990s in the Czech Republic, Lithuania and elsewhere resulted in reformed formulas that both contained a redistributional "internal" component, as well as an earning-related component. More recently, Croatia has moved half-heartedly in this direction in its first pillar formula for those joining the multi-pillar alternative. The redistributional component is based on the economy's average wage and years of work (or other service). These new benefit formulas replaced ones that gave greater weight to the first 20 years of work or other service and that contained higher accrual rates for women. Thus, the new formulas preserve some of the previous front-

---

[29] For a discussion of choice in designing multi-pillar pension regimes, see Palacios and Whitehouse (September 1998).

24

loading and bias toward women (who typically have lower lifetime earnings) but in a manner that arguably is more transparent and gender neutral.

In contrast the later Hungarian and Polish reforms contain first pillars and PAYG-only alternatives contain formulas that, with respect to future earnings, are linear across the earnings-distribution. In both countries, the political economy of pension policy in a post-socialist world was strongly away from continuing to maintain overtly redistributive pension formulas. Similarly, in Lithuania and the Czech Republic, retention of the redistributional component is a matter of continuing debate.

What seems to be preferred is what might be termed "alternative pension" formulas that target minimum pensions to longer service workers. These come in many varieties. In Poland, for example, workers with 20 (women) or 25 (men) years of work are entitled to a pension no less than 33 percent of average wage (this ratio will decline overtime). In Croatia, the minimum is more sensitive to marginal work effort: the minimum benefit varies between roughly 12 percent of a reference wage (average wage in 1998)[30] for someone with 15 years of work and increases by a factor of 0.825 percent per year, yielding a minimum at about 28 percent of average wage for someone with 35 years of work.

The jury remains out whether the "internal" or the "alternative" approach better achieves distributional objectives and at what fiscal costs.[31] A clear advantage to an alternative formula is that it simultaneously can serve the purpose of being a minimum pension guarantee in a multi-pillar system. But, as discussed below under the heading of guarantees, care has to be taken so that the alternative formula's design does not undercut the work and compliance incentives of the second pillar and the first pillar's underlying primary benefit formula. For example, a high minimum benefit that subsumes a large fraction of the workforce can compromise the incentives of a notional account reform with or without a second pillar.

Increasing effective retirement ages. In practice, a pension system's effective retirement age is the principal determinant of costs, adequacy and how effective its work and compliance incentives will be. In the face of increased life expectancy among the aged population, the only way to avoid either higher contribution rates or lower monthly benefits is to increase retirement ages, whether the system is financed on advance funding or pay-as-you-go principles. All other things being equal, an alternative minimum benefit, at the level that a country has determined is minimally adequate, will subsume a much smaller fraction of the population if effective retirement ages are higher.

Having actuarially neutral factors for early and delayed retirement in principle encourages work among the older population. Although similar results can be achieved

---

[30] Under the 1998 Croatian reform law, this 1998 reference wage may fall overtime; the law is not self-evident on this point. In addition, all departures from the norm of wage indexing currently are under legal and political challenge in Croatia.

[31] A country could have both a PAYG redistributional benefit formula and an alternative minimum benefit calculation that "tops up" the combination of results from the PAYG first pillar and the second pillar, as discussed under the heading of guarantees.

in conventional DB systems, the logic of notional accounts and the financial constraints of funded accounts may be useful in achieving that result. International experience does suggest, however, that the great majority of people will begin to draw benefits at the earliest possible age allowed, even in systems that contain actuarially neutral adjustments and reward work after the first age of eligibility.[32] The economic shock of transition has encouraged this behavior in most ECA countries. Even when there exists actuarial neutrality with respect to additional work after the first age of possible receipt, the availability of benefits itself has an offsetting income effect, especially among those who face liquidity constraints.

The combination of earnings tests for retirement and actuarially neutral factors arguably is more effective in encouraging individuals to work longer and delay receiving benefits, but such tests have their own negative effects on labor supply (especially among higher income households), are cumbersome to administer and in many ECA countries may exacerbate overall noncompliance in paying contributions and other taxes.

The most certain way to increase retirement ages is to increase the minimum statutory age at which benefits can be first withdrawn. This can be coupled with special funded account schemes (as in Bulgaria, Poland and Slovenia) to cover physically demanding or hazardous jobs and by generally adopting policies that accommodate voluntary savings to finance earlier retirement, at least with respect to an age range immediately below the statutory age in the mandatory system.

Increasing the initial age also helps assure that benefits will be more adequate at older ages. Compared to a system with lower initial ages for benefit receipt that has the same actuarial cost, one with higher initial ages is much more likely to pay benefits that meet and exceed commonly held norms of social adequacy.

Experience in the ECA region has been spotty on the issue of retirement ages. A few countries, notably Lithuania, took on the matter directly and relatively early on by eliminating early retirement privileges and beginning to gradually increase the regular retirement age. Georgia had to raise retirement ages by a full five years without any phase-in. Other countries have taken partial steps to eliminate early retirement privileges or transform them into private sector responsibilities. Countries that have legislated or are seriously considering multi-pillar reforms know that effective retirement ages have to rise for such reforms to be feasible. Delay in raising retirement ages can be costly. For example, both Croatia and Bulgaria, though they are now raising retirement ages quite aggressively, are doing so belatedly after dependency ratios are seriously deteriorated.

With few exceptions, ECA countries have not yet chosen to equalize male and female retirement ages. Over the longer haul, financing considerations, abetted possibly

---

[32] See Gruber and Wise (August 1997) for a discussion of incentives for early retirement in countries' state pension systems. See Diamond and Gruber (July 1997) and Coile and Gruber (April 2000) for a discussions of the US social security pension system, which system is more neutral than other universal state systems with respect to work after the first age of eligibility. The US case demonstrates that factors other than provisions of the universal state system, such as wide-spread employment-based occupational pensions and other forms of savings for retirement, can affect decisions as to when first to draw benefits.

26

by changing social norms and EU accession considerations, will keep resurfacing this issue.

Valorization and indexing rules. Benefits in the first pillar (or the PAYG alternative) need to have some predictability with respect to past wage histories. Even if the society is trying to achieve some gradual decline in replacement rates overtime, that glide path should follow predictable lines. In the interests of equity across workers with the same lifetime earnings and to prevent abuses in the setting of final salaries, it is best to determine benefits on lifetime wage histories, a goal toward which most ECA countries are moving. Wage histories have to be adjusted to reflect at least inflation over a worker's career. Typically this adjustment process -- often called "valorization" – uses growth in nominal wages over a worker's life and, so doing, takes into account productivity gains over that period. Recently, countries in the ECA region have departed from that standard norm in order to reduce replacement rates over time. Latvia, for example, uses growth in the annual "wage sum" (aggregate wages on which contributions have been assessed). In Poland, accrued rights from the old law system plus contributions paid under the new law are adjusted by 75 percent of average wage growth. In Croatia, wages effectively are being valorized by one-half wage growth and one-half price growth.

For the payment period, the adjustment process is conventionally labeled "indexing." During this period, the norm of predictability has to be weighed against financial constraints. If benefits are allowed to seriously erode in real terms, both the adequacy objectives are compromised and workers are not being given signals that their current contributions are buying them anything that has certainty associated with it.

Assuming finances permit, benefits should at least keep pace with inflation to assure adequacy goals are maintained. Inflation indexing can be mixed with a combination of average wage growth or wage sum growth depending on much the society wishes pensioners to share in both upside gains (for example, productivity and compliance increases) or downside risks (for example, recession and increased noncompliance).

In many of the ECA countries, growth in average wages had been the traditional standard by which benefits in pay status were adjusted. Switching to inflation or some combination of wage and price growth as the indexing norm is a means to reduce lifetime replacement rates, but this change should not be considered solely as a means to reduce short or long term costs by an expedient device. Over most periods for the same aggregate cost a society has the choice of higher initial replacement rates and price indexing at one extreme, and lower initial replacement rates and wage indexing as the other extreme. The latter alternative has the virtue of (most often) giving the elderly a benefit that increases in real terms over their retirement years during which other parts of their retirement portfolio may be eroding or being spent down unexpectedly. On the other hand, it not obvious that, given the realities of declining capacities in old age, individuals want their old age benefits to have the highest value the day they die.[33]

---

[33] This issue was addressed explicitly in the recent Swedish notional account reform. Rather receiving a typical wage-indexed PAYG annuity that starts at a lower real level and increases annually with both

3.4. Guarantees

A leading design issue is what will be the size of the minimum benefit guarantee for long-service workers. Many mandatory funded schemes (e.g., Chile) or multi-pillar systems (e.g., Hungary and Poland) have enacted a minimum benefit guarantee for long service workers, typically somewhere on the order of 25 to 35 percent of average wage (depending on the overall generosity of the system). This experience suggests that such a guarantee, while having many undesirable aspects, is inevitable and that first and second pillar design discussions should start with this issue and continuously return to it as the plan evolves.

A minimum benefit guarantee has implications in at least three areas. The first, noted earlier, is formal labor market incentives. In Chile the minimum applies to any worker with 20 years of participation. Some have argued that this encourages lower wage Chileans to participate in the formal pension system only long enough to qualify for the guaranteed minimum, and then work as legally exempt self-employed for the remainder of their work lives. This could render many of the incentive aspects of funded individual accounts a nullity. A notional account system with a generous minimum benefit, as in Sweden, may face similar problems.

One remedy is to make the required service period very long, such as 30 years, but this can lead to large inequities between those who for valid reasons only worked for 20 to 30 years. A more equitable and complicated remedy is to make the minimum benefit guarantee a function of years of work or other coverage. Thus, the minimum benefit guarantee might vary between 10 percent of average wage with only 15 years of coverage and top off at 25 percent of average wage with 30 years of coverage.

A minimum benefit guarantee also raises the second issue of why has an explicit pay-as-you-go first pillar. Aside from important risk diversification and distributional considerations, another answer is to minimize the state's contingent liabilities.[34] To the extent that the guarantee subsumes underneath it a fully funded scheme (such as in Chile) or even just part of a funded component in a multi-pillar system, the state faces future liabilities if outcomes from the funded pillar fall below the guarantee. The more the first pillar is likely to equal or exceed the guarantee, the less the state has in the way of contingent liability. This choice, of course, carries with it the burden of having to continuously finance ongoing PAYG liabilities. It is unclear from either experience to date or from theory whether over long periods expected costs of contingent liability are more or less than those of ongoing PAYG liabilities (which are also subject to future economic uncertainty). Much would depend on the details and incentives of the minimum benefit guarantee.

---

inflation and some measure of real growth, a Swedish retiree will receive a price-indexed annuity that is set at a higher initial level. This higher level "front loads" within it an *assumed* level of real growth in Sweden over the retiree's retirement life. To the extent that actual growth departs from the assumed path, retirees will receive annual adjustments that are more or less than price inflation. See Palmer (2000), page 6 for a helpful diagram.

[34] See Heller (1998) for a discussion of this trade-off.

The third matter raised by a minimum benefit guarantee is how much freedom overtime will be allowed pension funds to invest in more volatile assets or ones with higher default probabilities that nonetheless offer better return prospects. The greater the state's potential contingent liabilities, the more the regulator will hesitate in liberalizing investment rules. This could impede capital market development and thereby limit potential economic growth gains from funded pensions down the road.[35]

Guarantees on the absolute rate of return to be earned in the second pillar are the least desirable, particularly when, as in Hungary, the guarantee is tied to outcomes in the first pillar. The problems of trying to measure and reserve for such contingencies is causing Hungarian policy-makers to rethink this aspect of the 1998 reform laws.

Guarantees of relative rates of return, though popular, often had the undesirable consequence of encouraging all pension fund managers to hold essentially identical portfolios. The existence of such a guarantee removes any real choice that workers might otherwise have about how their retirement investment portfolio is structured. In the ECA context it is possible that countries, such as Poland or Hungary, with relatively large first pillars (whose outcomes equal or exceed adequacy norms in most instances) will loosen up the parameters in their relative return guarantees or even repeal them as their citizens gain more confidence in capital markets and risk-reward trade-offs.[36] In a country such as Croatia (assuming it implements its legislated second pillar), that flexibility may be harder to achieve because of the small relative size of the first pillar with respect to adequacy norms.

3.5. Disability and survivors benefits

Countries that have chosen to retain an explicit first pillar with an add-on mandatory second pillar have had to decide where to assign responsibility for disability (or invalidity) and survivors benefits.[37] These are benefits prescribed by law, and the designated survivors are the ones typically covered in most state pension systems (e.g., spouses, children, and dependent parents). So far in Central and Eastern Europe the decision has been to keep these benefits within the scope of the first pillar or pay-as-you-go pension. This is because the private insurance markets are relatively immature in these countries, and, accordingly, the preliminary judgment has been made that local (and even international) insurance companies are not yet prepared to take on either full or partial responsibility for providing these benefits.

In countries where disability and survivors benefits are handled by private insurance, it has been in the context of the privately managed pension funds performing multiple tasks: operating as investment fund of old age savings, the record keeper, a payer in the case of programmed withdrawals, and the purchaser of disability and term life insurance. The individual does not choose his disability or term insurer. Instead, his

---

35 For a good discussion of the 'political bind' posed by minimum benefit guarantees and contingent liabilities, see the recent Oxford Analytica, 2000.

36 In Sweden, where the first pillar is very large relative to the second pillar, there are no guarantees in the second pillar and investment options are largely unconstrained.

37 For more discussion of disability in a multi-pillar setting, see Arts and de Jong (September 1999).

or her pension fund purchases a group insurance contract that is periodically competed for the best price. In the event of disability or death, the insurer pays a defined benefit annuity based on prior earnings. The accumulation in the disabled or decedent's account reverts to the insurer to offset the cost of the disability or death benefit. In effect, the insurance contract "tops up" an individual's accumulation to the disability or death annuity levels prescribed by law.

If, instead, responsibility for disability and survivors benefits are assigned to the first pillar, the accumulations can either revert to the first pillar agency to hold down the costs of providing those benefits, or they can be additive to the statutory benefit provided by the first pillar agency. The former approach has the advantage of preventing a fiscal "leakage" relative to current law, thus permitting higher first pillar benefits or helping hold down contribution increases. So far the tendency in the ECA region has been toward what might be termed double benefits – households are entitled to full first pillar survivors and disability benefits from the public PAYG agency funds coupled with the households retaining rights to accumulations in the disabled's or decedent's funded account.

Partly this policy result occurred because disability and survivors' benefits were put on the backburner during the development of the overall pension reform scheme (for example, in both Hungary and Poland). By the time these design issues were confronted, decisions had been made that made it difficult to capture the accounts as a means of financing non-old age benefits, especially in the aftermath of the second pillar accounts being given the attributes of private property. It also may be inherently difficult to analogize a state agency with private insurance companies, particularly if the state PAYG agencies are not under public favor. In Croatia, however, second pillar accumulations would be used to offset survivors' and disability payments from the first pillar.

Once the new mandatory two pillar retirement system has been established with all the logistical operations specified and tested – exactly how, if any, central collection and record keeping operations will operate and how old age benefits shall be paid (e.g., will annuities be required and, if so, how) – the issue of where to assign disability and survivors benefits could be revisited. The survivor's function, for example, might be first shifted to insurance companies operating through group contracts negotiated by the pension funds. Providing disability insurance through the private insurance is a more problematic matter in terms of experience rating, administration and the application of social values. It should be noted, however, once the practice has been established of distributing second pillar accounts to households in the event of disability or death, it is probably impossible to require at some later date that the accounts must be paid over to insurance companies to defray costs. Accordingly, it incumbent for any country considering a multi-pillar system to think through this issue from a long-term perspective at the outset; it should not be left entirely to later resolution.

Survivor's benefits have two temporal dimensions. The first is the period before retirement, which was just discussed. The other is the period during which the accumulation is being drawn down as programmed withdrawals or as an annuity. Protection for surviving spouses in the second period can be provided by requiring married couples to draw down their old age accumulations in the form of an annuity that provides an survivors benefit ("joint and survivor" annuity). This was the decision in Croatia and Poland in designing its second pillar. Annuities and other payment options are discussed at greater length later.

Another matter that needs careful consideration is how disability and survivor's benefits will operate before and after the retirement decision so that no large differences in outcomes will occur. For example, in the case of an older worker (for example, someone aged 58-60), his or her first pillar disability benefit might be less than his first pillar old age benefit (based on years to date in the labor force) and the annuity value of his second pillar accumulation. In that instance, the law could provide for an election between the two benefit alternatives.

A final issue is that of inheritances, particularly in cases where no statutory legatees (spouses, children, dependent parents) exist. As discussed above, if second pillar accumulations revert to private insurers (or state PAYG agencies in lieu of private insurers) to defray the costs of providing legally specified survivors benefits, then already a substantial limit has been placed on the ability of individuals to transfer their accounts to beneficiaries of their own choosing. This also is the case if the accounts go to designated family members in addition to any first pillar benefit (such as spouses and children automatically inheriting second pillar accumulations).

But there are also instances of individuals dying before and after retirement with no current or past spouse, minor children or other dependent relatives covered by statutory provisions – for example, a middle aged divorced individual with a non-dependent former spouse and grown children. Typically second pillar schemes allow these moneys to go to whomever or to whatever institution the individual has designated. This, however, can constitute another leakage in the system that lowers available resources for either first or second pillar benefits. An alternative use of these funds is that they revert to the first pillar agency to lower the contribution costs of supporting the first pillar old age, disability and survivors benefits. Alternatively, if responsibility for survivor's benefits were assigned now or in the future to the pension funds, these amounts would revert to the pension funds to permit them to pay higher old age and survivors benefits to their members.

In sum, it is important to keep in mind and balance the "mixed" nature of second pillar accumulations, as presented in Figure One (page 12). The financing method and emphasis on individual accounts invokes standard notions of capital accumulation (for example, one's bank account), rather than insurance, even though insurance rights are also a form of property. But a system of accounts, the size of which is mandated by the government, where investment options typically are limited, and withdrawal options are generally defined is hardly "private property" in most commonsensical meanings of that term.[38] Such mandated accounts are part of a country's fabric of social insurance as much as PAYG rights. The private property aspects of second pillar accounts can be important in creating presumptions against governments using these monies for particular

---

[38] This sentence paraphrases a parallel observation about the possibility of funded accounts in the context of possible changes to the US Social Security old age, disability and survivors' program. (Penner, Sawhill and Taylor, 2000, page 144.)

investment ends and against many political default risks. On the other hand, if their social insurance aspects are excessively downplayed, overall costs may increase and key social objectives forgotten.

3.6. Second pillar pension funds

There are many ways to constitute and operate second pillar funds. They include entities that are closely connected with employers because the second pillar mandate technically falls on the employer or because employers can sponsor funds. Similarly unions can have different degrees of involvement. In general, the ECA countries have chosen to adopt an overall model from Latin America in which the funds are independent financial entities, not connected by a worker's place of employment or union membership. (The recent law in Bulgaria is an exception.) Each worker chooses his or her own pension fund, much like choosing one's bank. As noted earlier, this worker-choice model is thought to help insulate accounts from inappropriate political interference, and it is what is likely necessary to use pensions as the means to develop a country's internal capital markets and associated institutions.[39]

In organizing second pillar funds, it is desirable to have clear legal separation between the property rights and assets of fund managers and those of account holders. Within the practices and traditions of civil law countries, getting this result has not always been easy to achieve.[40] In some countries, such as Poland and Croatia, it has been possible to build on precedents established under their investment company laws. Under those laws, separate fund management companies and funds are created, but each fund is inexorably linked with a particular fund management company and is merely the sum of participants' accumulations (similar to a managed trust fund in common law countries). In other countries, such as Hungary, the solution was to create membership organizations (mutual benefit societies) that technically hire fund managers; many would-be fund management companies, however, founded membership organizations and executed long term binding contracts between themselves and the funds. In practice, outcomes have been the same, although it is argued that the former approach leads to more transparent accounting of costs.

In considering the organization of second pillar funds, some other particular issues typically arise. One is the role of life insurance companies; the other related one is whether second pillar rules should permit insurance companies to offer non-DC products. A third issue is whether a state sponsored fund should be allowed or even required, and a fourth is what kind of "default" arrangements should exist for those who do not choose a particular second pillar fund.

Role of life insurance companies. Life insurance companies, along with banks and investment fund sponsors, are experienced in managing investment portfolios, typically

---

For a very different approach to the organization and management of mandatory individual accounts, see Kotlikoff (August 1999).

[40] The usual solution in common law countries is use of the trust concept. Ironically, the concept comes into English law from Roman law first by way of canon law, enforced by conscience and Church tribunals, and later as part of Equity enforced by the King's Chancery Court.

of the type that are appropriate for second pillar funds. In the model generally adopted in ECA, insurance companies have become second pillar fund managers by means of organizing a legally separate affiliate. Because of their experience in international asset management, well-grounded insurance companies should be encouraged to enter a country's second pillar market, but they should not enjoy a favored position.

Deferred annuity contracts and guaranteed investment contracts. A much different issue has arisen in some countries – should life insurance companies be allowed to offer products that differ from a standard defined contribution account where the ultimate investment risk rests on the account holder (ignoring any state guarantees). These products probably would take the form of deferred annuity contracts in which individuals would be offered some minimum return on contributions during the accumulation period as well as the payment period. Another way of characterizing them is accounts for which the fund manager offers a guaranteed return during the accumulation period.

Allowing these products would complicate supervision and the transparency in comparing results across fund. In addition, annuities during the payment period and life insurance products often have industry or government guarantees associated with them. It might be impossible not to extend those guarantees to second pillar deferred annuity contracts as well. For these reasons, most advisors in the field have counseled against licensing these products during the accumulation period. This matter is a topic of ongoing lively debate in Estonia.

Fund Managed by the State. In a number of countries we have seen the emergence of a state-managed alternative to the second pillar fund. In some cases this fund was established as default option for those persons who fail to elect to have their funds placed with a private fund manager. In other cases, the state fund is a full-fledged competitor to the private funds. The success of the different initiatives is in many respects a function of the regard that the public has for the institution that founded the state fund.

In Mexico, for example, a subsidiary of the original state social security institution tries to compete with private fund managers, but without much success. In Kazakhstan the situation is a bit clouded and although the state accumulation fund has the largest share of the market, this is perhaps more due to the private funds not being a credible alternative in the Kazakhstan context.

State-managed pension funds generally do not have a good record.[41] Even if embedded in a environment of competing funds, managers of a state sponsored may be less able than private fund managers to resist (often subtle) political pressures to invest funds in a manner not in the best interest of participants. There is also a risk that the public will perceive that the fund enjoys a special guarantee of performance or a minimum rate of return due simply to the fact that the fund is managed by the state. On the whole, it is probably wiser not to conflict the role of the state as a supervisor with management of a pension fund.

---

[41] Palacios and Iglesias (January 2000).

Default options. For those in the age range in which participation in the multi-pillar scheme is an option, the default option is, of course, remaining in the PAYG-only scheme. For those for whom participation in the multi-pillar arrangement is mandatory, then, in the absence of any state fund as the default option, some rule has to be adopted for those who fail to make a choice.

One alternative is to assign individuals randomly to different funds, the approach chosen in Poland. Some other options may be possible. For example, before the second pillar funds have reached a reasonably mature size, it might be best to allocate 100% of the contributions of workers who do not make an election to a special fund invested entirely in government securities. Unlike a state-managed fund, this would be a passive holding fund within, for example, the central bank. Once funds have matured to some degree, then the assets in this holding fund would be apportioned out among the pension funds (or just the five leading funds) for management in accordance to their market share.

Once the funds are developed and achieved a sizable accumulation, the government may consider the proposed approach (or other options such as lottery) to allocated these contributions. The money accumulated in the interim should be re-allocated according to the same approach. Thus, if one fund has 25% of the assets held by all funds combined, then 25% of the money contributed by those who do not make an election would be allocated to this fund. These allocations would have to be adjusted periodically.

3.7. Administration

Collection and Clearinghouse design. With the exception of Hungary, the trend in the ECA region is to consolidate at least some aspects of second pillar operations with the operations of the state's first pillar agency or its tax authority. The phrase "clearinghouse" has come to encompass a variety of options on a spectrum that range from only using a state agency to collect second pillar contributions and allocate them among to second pillar funds, to being an alternative record-keeper, to being an exclusive record-keeper and information agent for fund participants. The arguments for consolidation include the following.

- *Economies of scale* gained as a result of operation of a single transfer agent.[42]
- *Reduction of burden on employers* to deal with more than one collecting entity.
- *Information barrier between employers and pension funds.* By funneling contributions through the first pillar agency (as in Poland) or the tax authority (as in Argentina), employers cannot know to which funds their workers are subscribing. This minimizes funds using employers as a means to pressure workers to sign up with one or the other fund.
- *Greater investment flexibility for second pillar participants.* Under a centralized registry structure, participants could divide their fund accumulations among qualified funds without administrative difficulty.
- *Information barrier between fund managers and fund participants that* can potentially reduce marketing cost and pressure. With a centralized registry, it would not be

---

[42] See Demarco and Rofman (1999)

necessary for fund managers to know the identity of their individual clients, as they would deal with the aggregate amount of assets lodged with it by the collector/registry. The fund would report to this entity the performance of the account and it would prepare statements and other reports for participants indicating to them from time to time the amount of units purchased and owned and the value of each unit.

In theory, this second "information barrier" between funds and their clients within a central registry system would greatly reduce emphasis on use of direct marketing to increase market share.[43] This direct marketing costs has led to very high costs of acquisition with a resultant decline in the value of the funds accumulated on behalf of clients. This kind of information clearinghouse is part of the Swedish and Latvian second pillars now being implemented. Any information clearinghouse would have to be included in a country's original second pillar design if it were to ever be successfully introduced. Once an industry of commissioned agents develops, it becomes a powerful lobby group against its extinction.

Figure 4: Combined Collection & Clearinghouse

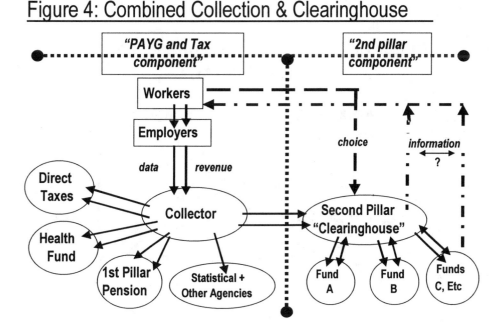

Figure 4 illustrates a unified revenue and data collection system, combined with integrated second pillar clearinghouse. The much debated issue of an information barrier between funds and clients is shown as an open question by having dual reporting lines

---

[43] See James, Smalhout and Vittas (1999) for a discussion of this aspect of administrative costs, among others. See Thompson (1999) for some stylized effects of administrative costs on benefit outcomes based the experience of several countries. See Whitehouse (June 2000) for an extensive discussion of empirical evidence and literature on the administrative charges associated with funded pensions.

back to workers and a question mark between those lines. A combined collection scheme can be created without a second pillar clearinghouse (left hand side of the diagram) in countries that do not have second pillars. In addition, as in Poland, the social insurance collection function may <u>not</u> be combined with the national tax authority, and instead it is the social insurance agency that operates as a full or partial clearinghouse for the second pillar funds. It is also conceivable that a second pillar clearinghouse could be created that operates independently of otherwise unified collection system, or even as a third independent collector, but such institutional arrangements would consume more real resources in terms of employer burden and state resources.

The efficiency advantages of consolidation have proven more elusive in practice than in theory. Neither Poland with its consolidation of first and second pillar collections nor Hungary with its decentralized second pillar model has a clearly better record, though employer burden remains a major unexamined element and both systems are in their infancy. The initial administrative failings in the both countries probably have more to do with inadequate time and resources devoted to implementation than the particular administrative approach chosen. The Hungarian decentralized model is shown in Figure 5.

FIGURE 5: DECENTRALIZED FUNDED PILLAR
(CHILE, HUNGARY)

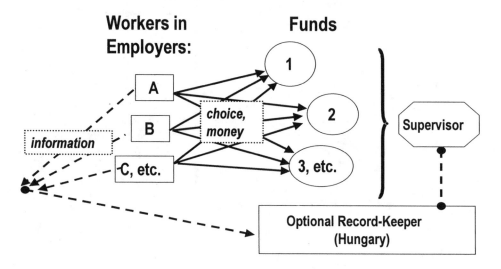

Though this decentralized model is quicker to implement, inherently it carries with it a greater transaction burden on employers; instead of having to deal with one or two potential collectors (tax and social insurance agencies), employers each must sort out second pillar contributions among a larger number of second pillar companies. Accordingly, the higher transaction costs to employers probably leads to a higher level of noncompliance, especially in terms of intra-year transmittal of contributions and data. Along with this additional burdens come opportunities for employers to try to influence workers' choices among funds. Hungary has attempted to counter those risks by building an independent record-keeper, but has encountered considerable systems problems in getting that activity established and functioning. In the meantime, responsibility for collection of social insurance contributions (including what is owed to the first pillar agency) has been transferred to the Hungarian tax authority, leading to the question of whether responsibility for second pillar contributions should also move. This would require, however, the tax authority having to deal with more frequent reporting about individual workers, and it would require the creation of a clearinghouse mechanism within, or affiliated by information linkages, with the tax authority.

As the previous discussion suggests, in many ECA countries, the clearinghouse issue is entangled with wider issues of more effective revenue collection and compliance. In many countries this means investing in the creation of at least one effective revenue collector. In this context it seems wasteful of real resources to create two or more separate revenue collectors for the withholding of direct taxes and social contributions at the payroll level of firms and the self-employed. Without the predicate of a credible revenue collector, it is uncertain that any first or second pillar pension system can be effective in coverage and fiscally viable in the long run.

Accordingly, the administrative aspects of any reform should start with a very careful assessment of the quality of current account numbering systems and information transfer systems. Above all and first in line, a clear national strategy must exist, or must be developed and implemented, concerning the enumeration of workers and their dependents (effectively all citizens), as well as employers. That strategy must include government-wide understandings at the highest level about the purposes and ownership of the one or more numbering systems (and linkages). Planners should assume that preparations for the reform would take at least two years from the time the legislation was enacted.

This caution also applies to other aspects of the reform. Successful implementation of a program of funded individual accounts requires extensive advance institutional development. Both local participants and outside observers of the reforms in Poland and Hungary can testify to the problems experienced in those countries as a result of inadequate implementation preparations. Offsetting these cautions, however, are the imperatives of building on key moments of political consensus and sometimes having to motivate settled bureaucracies. Arguably, messy reform is better than no reform. But administrative mess can discredit an otherwise meritorious reform at the outset and cause many workers to lose part of their initial pension contributions.

The strategy for collecting information on individual worker's contributions poses another challenge. Most second pillar pension systems require that contribution payments be deposited at least once each month. The systems differ in the timing of information reports, however.

Poland, Hungary and the individual account systems in Latin America require employers to report each worker's contributions each month. The social security systems in many of the most highly developed countries, however, including individual account systems in the U.K. and Sweden, rely on annual reports. The advantage of annual reports is that they reduce the reporting burden on employers and allow the processing agency to check more carefully that the reported information is accurate. The disadvantage is that long time lags are introduced between the collection of pension contributions and their transfer to the fund chosen by the worker. Under annual reporting, contribution payments probably would have to stay in some central holding account for about nine months on average before being transferred from the holding account to second pillar funds.

Monthly reporting eliminates the time lag, but generates such a large and continuing data flow that close checking of the data accuracy is almost impossible. The experiences in Poland and Hungary concerning monthly reporting have not been encouraging. In Poland, as of June 2000, 30 percent of the reports are found to have errors. The time and resources needed to correct the errors is delaying the entire reporting process. In Hungary, some employers simply ignore the rules to avoid the reporting burden. In particular, they submit required data and contributions less frequently than each month and often do not accompany money with data or visa versa.

In light of these experiences, countries considering second pillar schemes may wish to consider intermediate options, such as quarterly or biannual reporting. This would decrease the time money is held in any central holding fund (earning a government bond rate) but minimize the burdens on both employer and administrators flowing from monthly reporting.[44]

3.8. Government supervision of second pillar fund managers

Second pillar funds represent a very special type of financial institution. Contributions of participants are collected by government on a mandatory basis and then turned over to private sector managers. It is generally thought that funds of this nature should be subject to a higher level of protection than funds accumulated from the voluntary savings of individuals.

Supervisory agency. It is critical to establish a supervisory regime that adequately responds to the needs of participants in the second pillar pensions. This includes whether to assign supervision to existing agencies or to create a special supervisor. In resolving that issue, it is essential that the following commitments are kept foremost.

- The agency must have clear regulatory and enforcement powers, with authority to impose penalties to managers and even withdraw licenses if circumstances justify doing it.
- The staff of the agency should be well trained, with competing salaries to avoid losing them to the private industry.
- The agency should have an adequate budget, in order to operate without interference and have the necessary physical and technical resources.

---

[44] Any holding fund would pay at least the rate on government paper and could pay a rate equal to the average of the combined second pillar funds. In the latter case, workers would bear no material consequence of the transfer lag in terms of the value of their eventual accumulation and annuity value. This solution, however, would limit workers' choice among funds to some degree, and in many ECA countries, public confidence in the reform might be undercut if the government is seen as holding second pillar moneys for any length of time.

- Most important, the agency should be politically independent, to avoid interference with its activities.

If existing supervisory agencies – in particular the country's Securities Commission -- meet these requirements, then a reasonable option is to assign pension fund supervision to their functions. But if no existing agency clearly meets these standards, it may be necessary to create a new agency. (Alternatively, an existing agency might be totally revamped, but it is usually more difficult to change an existing agency's culture than to start a new one.)

Advisors coming from the Latin American experience generally have argued in favor of newly created separate agencies in order to allow the pension agency to concentrate on pension fund supervision to the exclusion of all else. If the state mandates individual accounts, then those accounts are, as noted earlier, a type of social insurance demanding special scrutiny. Further, in order to sell a novel reform to the public, it must be assured that these accounts will be supervised to an extraordinary degree. And it should be remembered that most of the publics in the ECA region have had to go through one or more banking crises and investment fund scandals over the past decade.

Weighed against the arguments for a separate agency are concerns about scarce human capital, the start-up costs and time attendant on creating a new agency and which configuration, in the ECA context, best avoids capture of the regulator by the regulated. In addition, in the ECA region, bilateral and multilateral technical assistance to nascent regulators of securities and exchanges has been considerable, providing a base in most countries on which to build. If too much emphasis is placed on the social aspects of the mandated accounts, the regulatory function may be assigned to a body affiliated with a social or labor ministry, which have little or not experience with financial markets and interests and views that are not always compatible with the logic of those markets. Further complicating this debate is the emergence in the ECA region of a wider and parallel debate as to whether financial market supervision should be generally consolidated.

Experience in the region is mixed. Hungary pioneered having a separate pension regulator, only to have it recently swallowed within an overall financial market regulatory agency. The Baltic countries have opted for assigning the task to their security regulators, mostly for scale reasons. On the other hand, for different political economy reasons and despite having credible securities commissions, Poland, Croatia and Bulgaria have opted for separate regulators. This choice has contributed to some start-up problems in Croatia and Bulgaria but not in Poland.

In terms of the organization of the supervisor, there are at least four areas of supervision that need to be covered, together with a department of planning or studies.

- The first one is responsibility for institutional control, including licensing, marketing and advertisement activities, disclosure of information by managers and pension funds, performance assessment and on site inspections.

- The second is responsibility for financial activities, including collection processes, custodianship, asset valuation; returns calculation, investment limits and, if any, minimum return guarantees. This area of responsibility involves collecting information from pension fund managers, custodians and the market, and cross checking these sources continuously.

- The third is responsibility for regulating and monitoring membership issues during the accumulation period – that is, the process to become member of a pension fund and switch to another one and the way pension funds communicate with their members. Vital to this area of responsibility is maintenance of a strong complaints department, capable of receiving, processing and solving complaints of workers against pension fund managers.

- The fourth is responsibility for benefit payments. This includes procedures to obtain benefits (lump sums, programmed withdrawals or annuities). This area of responsibility would concentrate on procedures to obtain benefits, annuity regulations and the ongoing supervision of benefit payments (including handling complaints). Depending on decisions about annuities, *some aspects of this area of responsibility could lie within the Insurance Regulator*, instead of the pension regulator (or securities commission), or within both regulatory agencies if both programmed withdrawals and annuities are options.

- The fifth and final area of responsibility is one for analysis and planning. This function should be responsible for strategic planning in the supervision agency, preparing and publishing statistical reports and studies on the evolution of the system, and developing new regulations.

Minimal capital. A key policy issue is the minimum capital to be invested by asset management companies in support of the second pillar operations. If a substantial minimum is established, only well managed companies that understand the business and can operate it effectively will enter the market. This capital requirement can be specified as a percentage of assets to be invested in the fund or as absolute amount. In Poland, the requirement is 4 million Euros.

Investment regulation. Fund regulations would also include controls on investments. This is a very complex question because of the fact that in transition economies the capital market is not yet well developed and the fact that there are no government securities in circulation. The appropriate measures to protect the savings of third pillar participants usually include rules to encourage diversification and to avoid concentration of risk. The objective is to obtain the maximum yield that is consistent with safety of the sums invested.[45]

Investments of private pension funds in are usually subject to limits that restrict participation in equities or other asset type, limit to avoid concentration by issuer (of all asset types) and rules to prevent, or at least minimize, the risk of investments with related

---

[45] See Demarco and Rofman (1998).

parties and any transactions that represent conflicts of interest. Successful reform efforts in other countries have normally begun with the application of restrictive rules that are later relaxed as the markets mature. To enforce prudential controls, there probably should not be investments in real estate for an initial period.

While it is not advisable to have any rules mandating a minimum investment in government paper, this is advice honored more in the breach -- despite experience that, for reasons of security and perhaps liquidity, most fund managers will include the investment of a substantial proportion of fund assets into government securities. At the very least, pension funds should only hold otherwise marketable government debt. Making pension funds captives of special government paper eviscerates any economic gains from the second pillar and arguably just repackages a country's existing implicit pension debt.

Another consideration is the proportion of assets that is to be invested outside the country. Often there is only limited scope for domestic investment, even in large countries such as Russia or Ukraine. Each country will have to weigh country risk diversification against the objectives of increasing domestic investment and increasing efficiency in its own capital markets.[46]

3.9. Second pillar retirement age and payment options

It is important to consider carefully the options that are provided to individuals who approach retirement and must decide what to do with the funds they have accumulated in their second pillar funds. Unfortunately, there exist no ideal models in operation from which to determine "best practice." Other options that might address the imperfections in what most countries have done exist either in theory or are just being tested.

Second Pillar Retirement Age. The general practice has been to apply first pillar retirement ages to when individuals can access their second pillar accumulations. An exception to this rule might be the case where the second pillar accumulation is quite large. Individuals might be allowed to early access to their accounts – for example, age 60 instead of age 63 – if the combination of the first pill[47]ar benefit and second pillar payment level at age 60 exceeds some measure such as 130 percent of what would be their benefits payable at age 63. While introducing undesirable complication into the system, this type of rule may be necessary in periods when rates of return have been exceptionally good and people wish to consume their unanticipated wealth in the form of early retirement. In Chile, Peru and Argentina, workers are allowed to take a lump sum withdrawal from their accounts provided they have purchased an annuity that provides them with a replacement rate of 70 percent.

---

[46] See Kotlikoff (August 1999) for one view on this matter.

[47] See Walliser (January 2000) for a discussion of policy arguments in favor of requiring annuities and desirable characteristics for any such required annuities. See also James, E. and Vittas, D. (September 1999) for some evidence about the operation of annuity markets across the world.

Choice between phased withdrawals and life annuities. Each of these two most common payment options has its advantages and disadvantages:

* The main drawbacks of phased withdrawal option are the risks of longevity and adverse selection. First, retired individual bears a longevity risk where he lives to an age when the full amount of money that has been accumulated is exhausted. In a situation where the government has guaranteed, either explicitly or by practice, some minimum replacement rate for retired workers, the government will find itself obliged to supplement the retirement income. In practice, a government guarantee does get triggered, creating uncertain and potentially large liabilities for future governments. Second, if annuities are not required, then insurance companies face the risk of "adverse selection" where only the relatively long lived choosing to buy annuities. Hedging against the selection risks can and does add to the price that insurance companies charge for annuities.

* Mandating annuities (as in Poland, Hungary and Croatia), on the other hand brings with it yet other problems. The key problem is the timing of when accumulations are converted to annuities. It is difficult to force a retiring cohort to purchase annuities in a down market. Some countries (such as the UK) allow grace periods in which individuals can defer the purchase of annuities. This, however, reintroduces adverse selection costs and can lead to leakage due to inheritance. The alternative of requiring individuals to convert over a five to ten year period before retirement has not been yet tested and has its own practical and interpersonal equity problems.

To solve some of these problems, as well as the pricing problems discussed below, proposals have been made to create "single annuity pools" to which accumulations would be diverted upon retirement (or on some phased basis before and after retirement). The problem with this scheme is who manages the annuity pool and will undue pressure be put on its managers to set mortality and interest rate assumptions to maximize benefit levels, especially at the beginning. A more complicated variation is to force successive cohorts to participate in "group annuities" that are purchased through international tender. While attractive in theory, this proposal has never been fully specified or tested.

Life annuities can be designed to provide certain protection for survivors. For example, common forms involve payments for the life of the retired worker but with a provision that payments will be continued for a minimum number of years to a designated survivor (the "certain" period) in the event of the premature death of the annuitant. Another popular option is a joint annuity payable to the worker and spouse, with payments continued until the death of the second of them ("joint and last survivor"). These life annuity options thus permit the worker to create a certain "inheritance" from the accumulated savings.

In a number of countries, policymakers have initially mandated settlement in only one of these forms, only to later conclude that participants should be given an option to select the option that best suits individual circumstances. In Colombia, for example, it is now common to also offer the option that combines phased withdrawals during an initial period following retirement, with the purchase of a deferred life annuity. So far, in the ECA region, mandated annuities has been the only chosen policy approach, but this may be reconsidered as the time for withdrawals approaches or later in the light of actual experience.

Pricing of Annuities. Increasing amounts of research and policy analysis is being devoted lately to the question of how annuities are priced. Life insurance companies price these contacts by making forecasts of longevity of workers and of future rates of investment return. In order to avoid placing themselves in a position where they will not be able to meet the promised annuity payments in future, they tend to be somewhat conservative in making these estimates. Experience in the UK has shown that it is very difficult to forecast longevity and even though actuaries have been making estimates of improvements in mortality as people seem to be living longer and longer, the estimated improvements in mortality have regularly been found to be less that the actual improvements.

Concerning the matter of rates of investment return, the situation is even more difficult. Annuity contracts are very long-term arrangements, and by definition there is a gradual depletion of the sums invested over the duration of the contract. It is almost impossible to find an investment that matches this liability profile. The problem is compounded when individuals seek to purchase a contract that guarantees in advance the rates of annuity for many years into the future. The life insurance company must forecast the investment earnings it can expect for 20 years or more in order to price such a contract.

A further complication arises when annuitants expect to receive benefits that are increased from time to time in line with changes in the cost of living. Such a contract, usually labeled "indexed annuities," has been developed in those markets where there is an ample supply of medium to long term investments available that offer real rates of return. In other words, the investments themselves must be regularly adjusted with changes in inflation. In an economy that does not have this type of securities, life insurance companies would not be prepared to offer such adjustable annuities.

Because countries often feel strongly that price-indexed annuities must be part of any funded pillar scheme, they are then required to help life insurance companies deal with investment uncertainty by issuing indexed bonds. This is a mixed blessing for governments and financial markets. To some extent, indexed bonds may improve efficiency in financial markets and lead to lower debt financing costs for governments. On the other hand, most governments find it hard to issue indexed bonds that have the same duration as annuities. Further, when a government issues indexed bonds, it imposes risks on future taxpayers that are very similar to those in a pay-as-you-go system, thus diminishing the risk diversification from a multi-pillar pension system.

4. Conclusions: "one size does not fit all"

While the above-described technical issues are critical for a good design of a multi-pillar system, some big choices need to be made before. The key choice is the shape of the desired pension system: should it be multi-pillar? Is it the right time to move to a multi-pillar system?

43

Initial conditions matter a lot in answering those questions. Some countries clearly have conditions conducive to an immediate introduction of the multi-pillar system. Other countries begin from a more precarious starting point, simply having very little resources. Figure 2 below illustrates these differences by plotting replacement rates against average monthly pensions in US purchasing power adjusted dollars. It is not surprising that the picture shows a positive correlation, but the striking element is the huge range of absolute pension levels in the region and therefore, the capacities of less affluent ECA countries to go beyond income support programs focused on the poor, at least in the short-term. The disparity is evident when we compare Georgia (at the bottom left-hand corner) with its 12 percent replacement rate on local income per capita and a monthly pension of 10 dollars with Slovenia, with replacement rates of about 50 percent and absolute average pension levels of almost 500 US dollars.

Figure 6: A wide range of absolute pension levels in the ECA region

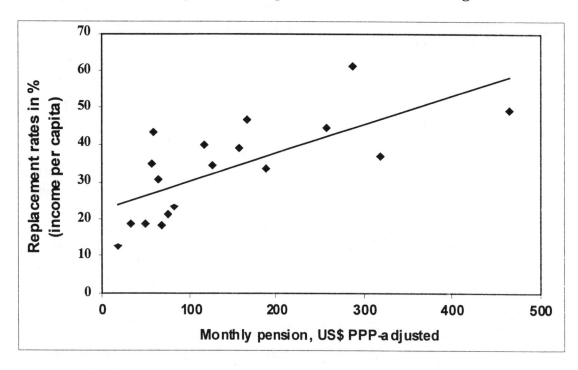

Source: Robert Palacios' analysis based on the World Bank data set.

In addition to the need to focus on poverty in the short run, the low pension and wage levels found in the countries in the bottom left hand corner of the figure make it difficult to enforce consumption smoothing programs, such as fully funded pillars of the pension system. Individuals would prefer low savings rates and will actively avoid compliance with forced savings schemes (as well as other taxes). This fact is reflected in the inverse correlation that exists between informality and incomes in the region. From the point of view, it would also be problematic (but not impossible) to start a multi-pillar system with such low income levels given the fixed cost element in administrative charges for individual workers. Finally, most of the challenges for multi-pillar reformers will be more difficult for poor countries to overcome.

In conclusion, in the poorer ECA countries, a short-term focus on paying pensions on time and on maintaining flat distribution of pensions seem appropriate. When the wages start growing those countries should consider a step-by-step movement towards a multi-pillar system, starting with a notional account system that has the microeconomic advantages of the funded pillar (incentives to work longer, actuarial adjustment of pensions) without having macroeconomic ones (such as increased saving rate or financial market development ultimately contributing to higher growth).

While any dividing line between groups of countries will be arbitrary, following Palacios, Rutkowski, and Yu (1999), a common sense suggests separating countries where an absolute pension level of 100 dollars has not yet been achieved. This line could be considered the threshold for thinking about quick introduction of a multi-pillar system. From the figure, this group would include Armenia, Belarus, Georgia, Kazakhstan, Kyrgyz Republic, Moldova, Ukraine, and Russia. Those with more than 100 dollar monthly pensions including Bulgaria, Croatia, Latvia, Lithuania, Slovakia, Poland, Hungary, the Czech Republic Romania and Slovenia. Not surprisingly, as discussed earlier, second pillars are being instituted primarily in European ECA countries, while the Caucasus and Central Asian ECA countries focus on first pillar reforms (with the notable exception of Kazakhstan).

The analysis above, as well as developments in practice, reflects the fact that in the process of thinking about pension reform there are two "decision thresholds". The first threshold is a decision on whether the country can afford consumption smoothing as the objective of the pension system. Here the proposed answer was described above, and the decisive factor appears to be the level of income. The second threshold is a decision about how to organize consumption smoothing. Consumption smoothing can be organized through a notional account scheme (Latvia, Poland, Kyrgyz Republic), a PAYG DB scheme with lifetime link between contributions and benefits (Lithuania, Moldova), multi-pillar systems (Hungary, Poland, Latvia) or almost entirely by funded pillars (Kazakhstan). The choice depends on country conditions: ability to run individual accounts (both notional and actual), ability to collect contributions in an efficient way, development of financial markets, the balance of the PAYG system, societal expectations, available financing of transition costs and others. One size does not fit all.

When the size is chosen, however, not every way of "wearing" the pension system works. The emerging dilemmas and practices examined in section three, show that the eventual success of pension reforms is sensitive to difficult policy and technical choices. The main lessons from that section are several. First, if funding is embraced, there should be clarity in why so: national savings, capital market development, household or country diversification. The design of the reform should follow from which objectives are paramount. Second, there should be clarity about financing the transition and how welfare losses and gains will be allocated overtime. Third, public policy infuses each and every aspect of the design of a funded scheme, even one that uses the form of individual accounts that have the attributes of private property. Deliberate policy choices have to be made about the timing and forms of withdrawal and about insurance for disability and death. Care has to be taken not to undermine the very labor incentives that individual accounts (and similar PAYG reforms) are designed to address by badly designed guarantees and their interaction with retirement age options. Attention has to be paid to a variety of costs and incentives, including collection and record keeping costs, burdens on employers, marketing incentives and costs. Finally, there are public administration challenges, certainly in supervision and probably in collection and "clearing," that demand careful planning, resources and time.

APPENDIX

To estimate the potential size of the offset, the following equation for a sample of 9 ECA countries, for which comparable data was available was estimated:

$$\frac{PExp}{GDP} = [\frac{TPen}{TPop} \times \frac{1}{LFP * (1-U) * FSP}] \times [\frac{AvgP}{GDP.per.FW}]$$

where:

PExp – Total national pension expenditures;
GDP – Gross Domestic Product;
TPen – Total number of the pensioners (including old-age, disabled, survivors)
TPop – Total population number;
LFP – Labor Force Participation rate;
U – Unemployment rate;
FSP – Formal Sector Participation rate;
AvgP – Average pension (covering old-age, disabled, survivors);
GDP.per.FW – GDP per formal worker.

The first bracketed expression represents effective dependency ratios, where demographic dependency (the first component) is modified to account for employment in the formal sector. In the second bracketed expression real GDP per formal worker, or average labor productivity, represents a proxy for the formal average wage in the economy. Consequently the ratio of the average pension to the average formal productivity approximates the average system replacement ratio (pension to wage).

The basic scenario assumes no change in key program variables over time and that the current ratios of average pension to average wage are maintained. What is more important, the baseline assumes that current benefit coverage rates persist over the forecast period.

In the ECA region, a very large percentage of today's retirees are covered by the formal state pension system, reflecting the very high levels of labor force participation and contribution coverage that existed under centrally planned economies. If we were to allow future benefit receipt to fall in accord with the drops in labor force participation that have occurred in the 1990s, our projections of future pension spending would be much smaller. In that event, however, we would be projecting and ignoring coverage gaps in 2050. Arguably, most ECA countries would not tolerate such coverage gaps to fully take hold and instead would create noncontributory pensions to compensate.[48] Those noncontributory pensions might take many forms: expanded means-tested

---

[48] In Lithuania, the unwillingness and inability of those in the rural sector to pay contributions for even a very low flat rate basic pension has led to debates as to whether to replace that component of Lithuania's 1994 pension reform with a noncontributory citizens' pension of an equivalent amount. This condition already has led the government to subsidize the farmers' contributions for the basic pension in the amount of 50 percent of the contribution for the basic pension. In Poland, farmers are covered by a similar flat rate pension that is 95 percent subsidized.

assistance at generous levels (as in Germany), *de jure* age related demogrants or citizens' pensions (as in New Zealand), or *de facto* citizens' pensions that rest on token contribution requirements from cash poor segments of the society (as in Poland's pension system for its rural sector). These alternative pension arrangements, however, likely would have somewhat lower average replacement rates than now exist in more formal contributory schemes, and to that extent our projections overstate future costs as a percent of GDP.

Offsetting that bias is another inherent assumption in our projections – that assessable money wages on which pensions are based -- does not grow as a percent of GDP overtime. This second assumption understates growth in pension spending in GDP terms but not in terms of payroll (required contribution rates).

We then estimated the relative contributions to pension expenditure of mortality, fertility, labor force participation, unemployment, formal sector participation, retirement age, and indexing rules were estimated. In doing the estimations, we started with the 2050 projected expenditure level and changed each factor holding all others constant, and observed the resulting relative change in pension expenditures in each case. An alternative evaluation first assumed that all the factors would change over time, and then to evaluate magnitude of each individual effect, each factor was switched off one by one. Differences in results between two approaches may arise as a consequence of numerous joint effects, and, accordingly, an average was taken as approximation of the expected magnitude of the individual effect of each factor.

In general, the assumptions about changes in parameters were as follows:

- **Mortality** was assumed in 20 years to approach current levels in Netherlands for each cohort;
- Total **Fertility** was assumed to change from the current levels in accordance with the projections from the US Census Bureau, as presented in the Appendix;
- **Labor force participation rate** (LFP) was expected to gradually increase in 50 years to the pre-transition levels;
- **Unemployment** was allowed over the period of 50 years to decrease to 50% of the current levels in each country;
- **Formal Sector Participation** (FSP) was assumed to expand to 90-95% from the current levels over the period of 50 years;
- **Retirement Age** was assumed to be raised to 65 for both men and women, in 7 years for men and more gradually for women.
- **Rules of indexing** of pension growth to real productivity growth *during the payment period* assumed 3 different schemes: 100% productivity growth (inherent in the baseline), 100% inflation in prices plus 50% of real productivity growth, and only 100 percent inflation in prices.

With the possible exception of the mortality improvement assumption, the assumptions about fertility, retirement age and indexing are fairly standard. Arguably not all of the ECA countries in the sample will see their mortality improve to today's Netherlands' level, although in light of trends in Western Europe, this is not an unreasonable benchmark. Note that the assumption is that these ECA countries still lag behind the Netherlands as that country's mortality continues to improve over the next fifty years. As far as labor market variables are concerned, the assumptions are a drop in unemployment by half, and a return of labor force participation generally and in the formal sector particularly to roughly pre-transition levels (see also main text).

As noted earlier, our projections do not take into account probable changes in the ratio of money wages to GDP over the period. Many ECA countries have money wage/GDP ratios that are low compared to most developed countries, and those ratios are almost certain to increase over the forecast period. Keeping this ratio at current levels over the projection period understates the size of future pension spending as a percent of GDP. It also equally affects the size of future contributions as a percent of GDP. Accordingly the measured effects we observe from changes in labor market factors would not be affected, aside from some minor timing effects.

Given our methodology, these labor market changes translate into changes on the revenue side of the equation, not the spending side. As noted, we implicitly assume that current rates of benefit coverage remain. If one treats these figures as indicative of what the political economies of ECA countries require them to spend on pensionable populations in any event, then they also indicate the magnitude of the revenue gains likely from increased economic activity and better compliance, regardless of particular tax bases, to match those spending imperatives. That is, for the same growth in economic activity and compliance, even if coverage in the country's formal contributory pension system has contracted and contribution revenues are therefore smaller, the country's income taxes arguably could be that much higher to finance noncontributory benefits.

Now we move to the presentation of the details of projections at the country level. The following table summarizes general characteristics of the countries of our sample:

1997-1998	Azerbaijan	Croatia	Estonia	Kyrgyzstan	Lithuania	Moldova	Poland	Russia	Ukraine
Total population	7,949,300	4,572,470	1,445,380	4,634,900	3,704,000	4,317,500	38,660,420	146,327,600	50,195,200
Number of pensioners	1,010,725	960,000[b]	360,000	542,500	780,000	743,500	9,332,000[a]	38,517,000	14,500,000
as % of statutory retirement age population	114%	96%[b]	126%	121%	100%	108%	170%[a]	127%	125%
Pension Expenditures, % GDP	3.3%	8.6%[b]	8.7%	6.5%	6.1%	7.4%	14.2%[a]	6.9%	9.3%[c]
Standardized LFP, total[e]	73%	52%	67%	64%	68%	69%	62%	68%	71%
Unemployment Rate, total	6%[d]	14%	10%	6%	12%	13%	10%	13%	11%
Dependency Ration[f]	29%	62%	63%	32%	48%	41%	59%	60%	63%
Effective Dependency Ratio[g]	44%	73%	68%	49%	52%	63%	69%	71%	82%

Notes:

a - including farmers;

b - including orphans / excluding military and family

c - on the cash basis;

d - assumed;

e - number of the employed in the age group of 15-70 divided by the number of population in the same age group.

f - ratio of pensioners to total workers, times 100%

g - ratio of pensioners to estimated number of formal workers, times 100%

To project values of the pension expenditures share in GDP, an Excel spreadsheet model was developed. The model produces set of matrices in dimensions of 52 by 200 (52 years, 100 cohorts of males and females) and uses the following data as inputs: current population structure, fertility and mortality rates, sex ratio at birth, labor force participation and unemployment rates, formal sector participation rate, statutory retirement age, ratio of the actual number of pensioners to the population in retirement age, current GDP, current average pension or pension expenditures.

The base year was taken 1998 for which most of the data was available; when in some cases data for certain indicators for 1998 was not available, data from 1997 or 1996 was applied.

The model consists of two modules – "demographics/labor" and "finances". Within the first module, given data on current population structure by age and gender and data and assumptions on mortality rates by age/gender and fertility rates by age of mother, population matrix for 50 years was generated. With data and assumptions on labor force participation, unemployment, and formal sector participation rates, matrix of the employed in formal sector was added. Also based on the data on current pensioner numbers and assumption on expected change in pension age together with the assumption about constant ratio of the number of pensioners to the number of retirement age population, the total number of pensioners for every year was projected. Effective dependency ratio as total number of pensioners over total number of formal employed was then calculated.

Within the second module, with data on current GDP, current value of the average formal productivity was obtained (GDP divided by number of formal workers). Then an assumption that its growth will gradually approach 1% in 2005 and will remain on that level until 2050 was introduced[49]. As a baseline, the average pension was assumed to grow at the same rate as average productivity. Alternatively we evaluated effects of policy when average pension growth was only half of the productivity growth and when average pension did not grow at all (essentially price indexing). The analysis was performed in real terms. Our baseline scenario relative to which all the effects were evaluated assumed the following:
   - current population pyramid evolving over time with unchanged parameters;
   - unchanged fertility & mortality rates as well as sex ratio at birth;
   - unchanged pension age:
         55/60 – for all countries, except:
         56/61 – for Estonia
         60/65 – for Poland
   - constant ratio of the number of pensioners to the number of retirement age population;
   - constant replacement rate (real benefits and real average productivity have the same growth rates);

---

[49] In fact, assumption about growth of average productivity becomes important only when we assume that average pension grows less than one-to-one with average productivity. It does not affect our baseline where we assume that pension will grow with productivity, in which case replacement ratio stays constant anyway. With higher productivity growth, less-than-one-to-one response of average pension will result in lower pension expenditure, however it will also cause more rapid deterioration of replacement ratios.

- implicit assumption is that coverage remains the same over the whole time horizon, which given its high current level and our assumption about formal sector participation expansion is quite reasonable.

Mortality rates

Original data on mortality levels, defined as ratios of number of people died in specific age to total number of population of that age cohort, was obtained from various countries' and World Bank sources. For the purposes of comparison of that statistics, respective life expectancies were calculated as presented in the table below. To evaluate

Mortality tables sources

	Year	Source	Calculated life expectancy (Total/M/F)
Azerbaijan	1997	State Statistical Committee	74/ 69.6/ 79
Croatia	1995	WB data	72.7/ 67.7/ 78.7
Estonia	1998	WB data	72.3/ 65.4/ 80.3
Kyrgyzstan	1997	WB data	68.1/ 62.8/ 74.3
Lithuania	1995	WB data	70.6/ 65.4/ 76.3
Moldova	2000	WB estimates	67.6/ 63.6/ 72.1
Poland	1991	calc. from US Census Bureau data	73.1/ 67.7/ 79.6
Russia	1998	State Committee of Statistics	68.5/ 61.6/ 76.3
Ukraine	1996	State Committee of Statistics	68/ 61.5/ 75.4
Netherlands (2020 target)	1996	Authors	77.8/ 75.1/ 80.8

the possible effect of mortality change, gradual conversion of the mortality rates over the period of 20 years in each country to the current levels in one of the West European countries was assumed. As a target value for mortality change, we set mortality rates for Holland as also indicated in the table below. So, our implicit assumption was that in twenty years life expectancy in all countries of the region will reach levels of 75.1 for men and 80.8 for women and will remain there until 2050.

Fertility rates

The original data on fertility rates defined number of children born by 1000 women of each specific age group. With this information total initial fertility rates were calculated

Current and expected fertility rates

	Azerbaijan	Croatia	Estonia	Kyrgyzstan	Lithuania	Moldova	Poland	Russia	Ukraine
1997-1998	2.11	1.69	1.21	2.76	1.39	1.60	1.51	1.24	1.31
2005	2.44	1.92	1.32	3.05	1.49	1.81	1.39	1.38	1.40
2020	2.38	1.85	1.64	2.66	1.80	2.03	1.49	1.70	1.71
2050	1.79	1.70	1.53	2.25	1.56	1.60	1.70	1.54	1.54

Source: 2005-2050 U.S. Bureau of the Census, International Data Base.

as presented in the table below for 1997-1998. Then with data on projected total fertility rates from US Census Bureau, total fertility adjustment coefficients for each year were calculated, assuming gradual change in total fertility rates over time between the specified years. In fact, with our time horizon our primary interest is in fertility dynamics until year 2030. Children born after that year will only start entering labor force in 2050 or will still remain below working age then.

Labor Force Participation and Unemployment rates

Data on current labor force participation (LFP) rates comes from national countries' and international sources, including U.S. Bureau of Census International Data Base. When quality of data on LFP was not satisfactory, we introduced certain adjustments to make sure that when applied these rates would generate the same total size of the labor force as indicated by national/international statistical sources for respective selected year.

Labor Force Participation Rates, current and 2050 projected

Country	Current total LFP rates		Method for obtaining 2050 age/gender specific LFP rates	Generated total new LFP rates with the same (1998) population structure		Generated total new LFP rates with 2050 population structure	
	M	F		M	F	M	F
Azerbaijan	84%	62%	Total LFP adjustment to 1991 value	89%	69%	88%	67%
Croatia	58%	47%	Slovakia 1993	77%	63%	73%	62%
Estonia	74%	61%	Total LFP adjustment to 1991 values	81%	69%	78%	66%
Kyrgyzstan	69%	59%	Kazakhstan 1989	79%	69%	79%	68%
Lithuania	72%	65%	Total LFP adjustment to 1993 value	75%	69%	74%	68%
Moldova	74%	64%	Romania 1996	79%	71%	78%	68%
Poland	69%	56%	Poland 1990	76%	62%	74%	60%
Russia	75%	62%	Russia 1989	80%	71%	74%	65%
Ukraine	75%	67%	Ukriane 1989	79%	73%	76%	69%

To test optimistic assumptions about labor market improvements, gradual converge of the labor force participation rates within 50 years to pre-transition levels was simulated. In cases where historical pre-transition data on LFP was not available, either highest recent LFP rates of a neighboring country were applied, or transformed current LFP rates were calculated in such manner that when applied they would generate total labor force of the size relative to the total population size specified by national statistics for 1989-1991. The fact that with increase of pension age there would probably be gradual expansion of labor force participation of transition cohorts (60-64 for men / 55-64 for women, in Poland for women of 60-64 only) it is natural to assume participation of the older workers (currently of retirement age, and later of working age) at least not to drop below the current levels. Additional increase in LFP rates for these transition cohorts was incorporated so that for most countries, our targeted participation rates for aged of 60-65 in 2050 varied in ranges of 50-60% and 40-50% for men and women respectively. With such expansion of LFP rates for transition cohorts of the elderly, the total effect on the aggregate participation rates varied only within 1-2%.

Since countries have different specifications for calculating LFP rates, a uniform standard had to be assumed. In all our reports total LFP rates define ratios of the employed population of the age 15-70 over the total number of population between 15 and 70. The following table summarizes the data and methods for obtaining targeted LFP rates.

Indicated new LFP rates also incorporate adjustment for increase in participation of the transition cohorts.

It was also assumed that within 50 years unemployment would gradually shrink to 50% of the current levels in each country.

Formal Sector Participation rates

Formal Sector Participation rates in most cases were estimated from a comparison of the national survey statistics on total employment with the official employment registry data and/or data on number of the contributors to pension fund. Countries were aggregated in the groups with average estimate of the indicator for the whole group. An assumption was made that in 50 years FSP rates for countries with comparatively low current levels would gradually converge to 90% and for countries with higher current levels they would converge to 95%, as indicated in the table below. Figures presented in the table and used in calculations are more indicative rather than exact estimates.

Indicators of Formal Sector Participation Rates

	current FSP average estimates	2050 targeted values
Azerbaijan, Kyrgyzstan, Moldova	65%	90%
Ukriane	77%	95%
Croatia, Lithuania Poland, Russia	85%	95%
Estonia	92%	95%

Example of evaluation of the individual effects of mortality and fertility

Table below presents sample evaluation of the effects of fertility change over time and mortality decrease for Russia. Two alternative methods are applied and their simple average is taken as the best estimate of the expected effect. Estimated individual effect represents magnitude of relative contribution of certain factor change into value of the pension expenditures in 2005 or 2020 or 2050 respectively.

Russia		Pension Expenditure in GDP, %			Estimated effect		
		2005	2020	2050	2005	2020	2050
	nothing changes	0.066	0.086	0.136			
off/on	only mortality on	0.067	0.097	0.181	1.4%	12.6%	32.3%
	only fertility on	0.066	0.086	0.116	0.0%	-0.1%	-15.1%
	everything changes*	0.063	0.084	0.112			
on/off	except mortality	0.062	0.075	0.085	1.4%	12.4%	31.5%
	except fertility	0.063	0.084	0.129	0.0%	-0.1%	-13.4%
average effect	mortality				1.4%	12.5%	31.9%
	fertility				0.0%	-0.1%	-14.3%

* - mortality, fertility, LFP, Unempl, FSP change over time according with the assumptions.

References

Barr N. (2000). "Reforming Pensions: Myths, Truths, and Policy Choices", Fiscal Affairs Department, International Monetary Fund, Washington DC, mimeo.

Brooks, S. and James, E. (September 1999). "The Political Economy of Pension Reform", version available on website for World Bank Conference "New Ideas About Old Age Security," volume forthcoming.

Chlon, A., M. Gora, and M. Rutkowski (August 1999). "Shaping Pension Reform in Poland: Security through Diversity", Social Protection Discussion Paper, No. 9923, August, The World Bank.

Coile, C. and Gruber, J. (August 2000). "Social Security and Retirement," NBER Working Paper No. W7830, National Bureau of Economic Research.

Demarco G. and R. Rofman (December 1998). "Supervising Mandatory Funded Pension Systems: Issues and Challenges", Social Protection Discussion Paper No. 9817, The World Bank.

Demarco G. and R. Rofman (February 1999). "Collecting and Transferring Pension Contributions", Social Protection Discussion Paper No. 9907, The World Bank.

Diamond, P. and Gruber, J. (July 1997). "Social Security and Retirement in the U.S.", NBER Working Paper No. W6097, National Bureau of Economic Research.

Disney, R. (August 1999). "OECD Public Pension Programmes in Crisis: An Evaluation of the Reform Options", Social Protection Discussion Paper No. 9921.

Fox, L. and Palmer, E. (August 1999). "Latvian Pension Reform", Social Protection Discussion Paper No. 9922, The World Bank.

Fox, L. and Palmer, E. (June 2000). " New Approaches to Multi-Pillar Pension Systems: What is the World is Going On?", version available on website for World Bank Conference "New Ideas About Old Age Security," volume forthcoming.

Geanakoplos, J., Olivia Mitchell and Stephen P. Zeldes, (1998). "Would a Privatized Social Security System Really Pay a Higher Rate of Return," *Framing the Social Security Debate: Values, Politics and Economics,* R. D. Arnold, A. Munnell and M. Graetz, eds., National Academy of Social Insurance, The Brookings Institution Press, pp. 137-156.

Gora, M. and M. Rutkowski (October 1998). "The Quest for Pension Reform: Poland's Security through Diversity", Social Protection Discussion Paper No. 9815, The World Bank.

Government of Poland, Office of the Government Plenipotentiary for Social Security Reform (June 1997). "Security Through Diversity: Reform of the Pension System in Poland", Warsaw.

Gruber, J. and Wise, D. (August 1997). "Social Security Programs and Retirement Around the World: Introduction and Summary of Papers", NBER Working Paper No. W6134, National Bureau of Economic Research.

Heller, P. (1998). "Rethinking Public Pension Reform Initiatives", IMF Working Paper WP/98/61, International Monetary Fund.

Herbertsson, T.T., J.M. Orzag, and P.R. Orzag (May 2000). "Retirement in the Nordic Countries: Prospects and Proposals for Reform," prepared for the Nordic Council of Ministers, available from Birkbeck College website at http://www.pensions-research.org

Holzmann, R. (1997). "Starting over in Pensions: The Challenges Facing Central and Eastern Europe", *Journal of Public Policy* 17, 3, pp. 195-222.

Holzmann, R. (December 1998). "Financing the Transition to Multipillar", Social Protection Discussion Paper No. 9809, The World Bank.

Holzmann, R. (2000). The World Bank Approach to Pension Reform, *International Social Security Review* 53, No. 1, 11-34.

Holzmann, R., T. Packard, and J. Cuesta (January 2000). "Extending Coverage in Multi-Pillar Pension Systems", Social Protection Discussion Paper No. 0002, The World Bank

Holzmann, R. (May 2000). "Can Investments in Emerging Markets Help Solve the Aging Problem?", Social Protection Discussion Paper No. 0010, The World Bank.

Milanovic, Branko (1998). Income, Inequality, and Poverty during the Transition from Planned to Market Economy, The World Bank, Washington D.C.

Oxford Analytics (2000) - Brief of June 12, 2000: 4, "INTERNATIONAL: Pension Reform" and "SUBJECT: The real macroeconomic effects of pension reforms in emerging markets."

Palacios, R. (December 1998). "A note on diversification between funded and PAYG pension schemes", mimeo available from author.

Palacios, R. and Iglesias A. (January 2000). "Managing Public Pension Reserves Part I: Evidence from the International Experience", Social Protection Discussion Paper No. 0003, The World Bank.

Palacios, R. and M. Pallares-Miralles (April 2000). "International Patterns of Pension Provision", Social Protection Discussion Paper, No. 0009, The World Bank.

Palacios, R. and R. Rocha (April 1998). "The Hungarian Pension System in Transition", Social Protection Discussion Paper No. 9805, The World Bank.

Palacios, R., M. Rutkowski, and X. Yu (1999), "Pensions Strategy Paper for Transition Economies, mimeo, The World Bank.

Palacios, R. and E. Whitehouse (September 1998) "The Role of Choice in the Transition to a Funded Pension System", Social Protection Discussion Paper No. 9812, The World Bank.

Palmer, E. (June 2000) "The Swedish Pension Reform Model: Framework and Issues", Social Protection Discussion Paper No. 0012, June 2000, The World Bank.

Rutkowski, M. (1998) "A New Generation of Pension Reform s Conquers the East - A Taxonomy in Transition Economies", *Transition*, vol. 9 (August), no. 4.

Thompson, L. (1998) Older and Wiser: The Economics of Public Pensions, The Urban Institute Press, 1998.

Whitehouse, E. (April 1999) "The Tax Treatment of Funded Pensions", Social Protection Discussion Paper No. 9910.

World Bank (1994) Averting the Old Age Crisis: Policies to Protect the Old and Promote Growth, Oxford University Press.